Life in the Shadows
of the Crystal Palace, 1910-1927

Life in the Shadows
of the Crystal Palace, 1910-1927:
Ford Workers in the Model T Era

Clarence Hooker

Bowling Green State University Popular Press
Bowling Green, OH 43403

Copyright © 1997 Bowling Green State University Popular Press

Library of Congress Cataloging-in-Publication Data
Hooker, Clarence.
   Life in the shadows of the Crystal Palace, 1910-1927 : Ford workers
in the model T era / Clarence Hooker.
      p. cm.
   Includes bibliographical references (p.   ) and index.
   ISBN 0-87972-737-3 (clothbound : alk. paper). -- ISBN 0-87972-738-1
(pbk. : alk. paper)
   1. Automobile industry workers--Michigan--Highland Park. 2. Ford
Motor Company--Employees. 3. Ford Model T automobile. 4. Ford,
Henry, 1863-1947. 5. Ford family. 6. Automobile industry and trade--
United States--History. I. Title.
HD8039.A82U6465 1996
331.7'6292'0977433--dc21   96-37556
                                                 CIP

Cover design by Dumm Art

Dedicated to the pioneers of the automotive industry,

especially the workers who lived in the vicinity

of the Crystal Palace and made the Model T Ford.

Contents

Introduction

Scholars devoted to the study of the history of Detroit and the automotive industry have recently called for a change in focus. Stephen Meyer, for example has noted that while biographies and autobiographies of the emperors and barons of the automotive industry abound, the histories of the workers have not been written. In stark contrast to the history of the barons, which has been given so much attention, the history of automotive workers such as those who lived and worked in the shadows of Ford's Highland Park plant (i.e., the Crystal Palace) remains hidden in the corners of the shops and departments throughout the automotive belt.[1] Nora Faires is among those who have made a call for a change in the focus of studies aimed at elucidating the social history of Detroit and the automotive industry.

In her recent review essay, Faires concludes that the books of Steve Babson, Meyer, and Olivier Zunz all added to the limited understanding of Detroit's ethnic groups of the late nineteenth century: "[T]he influx of foreign born workers of the Highland Park plant undergirds Meyer's discussion of the changing policies implemented in the factory; the shifting fortunes of the city's immigrant groups is the centerpiece of Zunz's analysis, and accounts of immigrant workers weave through Babson's saga."[2] But the important point is that "despite each author's concern with ethnic issues, the thinness of the secondary literature shows through the books, diluting their descriptions of the city's changing ethnic mosaic."[3] Given her special interest in women's history, Faires is most emphatic in noting that "the paucity of research on the lives of the city's women and the isolation of women's history form the mainstream of social history impoverishes all three books."[4] It is in the final paragraph of her authoritative critique, that Faires argues that the full historical reconstruction of Detroit's past will require that we know more about domestic servants, beauticians, waiters, and janitors; more about those outside the paid labor force, such as those tending children, the unemployed, and the aged; and more about various neighborhoods in the vast urban expanse, from the central city to the suburb.

Clearly it is time to focus on the anonymous men, women, and children whose energy fueled the industry, and whose collective biography is hidden in a variety of statistical reports, personnel department narratives, and (perhaps) in Upton Sinclair's *The Flivver King*. It is time to analyze Detroit in terms of the larger regional context—Wayne County and the surrounding counties out of which Detroit was carved. And, at the same time, it is necessary to consider how various neighborhoods and suburbs within the vicinity were influenced by the growing pains of Detroit and the automotive industry. As Sam Bass Warner and Sylvia Fleisch assert, it is time to ask, "What is the changing distribution of population and economic activities within a changing area" and by inference, where did Highland Park and the Crystal Palace fit into the settlement and cultural patterns of Detroit, Wayne County, Michigan, and the region.[5]

Olivier Zunz's *The Changing Face of Inequality: Urbanization, Industrial Development and Immigration in Detroit, 1880-1920*, has been a major influence in my thinking about how to analyze the symbiotic relationship between the Crystal Palace (i.e., the Ford Motor Company's presence) and the community and the Highland Park community. Recognized as a modern classic, Zunz's study has shown the relationship of industrial growth and changing patterns of inequality but has not specified the impact of particular industries or plants on the neighborhoods in which they were located. Utilizing a variety of sophisticated statistical and sampling techniques, and focusing on industrial expansion, land use patterns, and inter-ethnic social mobility, Zunz's work builds upon earlier studies (among which David Katzman, Stephen Thernstrom, and Forrester B. Washington's works are prominent),[6] and an impressive array of primary materials. Among Zunz's most important findings is that, by 1920, race and class had replaced ethnicity as the best explanation of inequality in Detroit: "[T]ranslated into the city's space, inequality took many faces, from largely self-imposed segregation of the nineteenth century ethnic communities, to the enforced segregation of blacks in the twentieth century."[7]

Generally speaking, Zunz's work is important because it adds to our understanding of the relationship of race, ethnicity, and class to industrial growth in twentieth-century Detroit; as a methodological guidebook it is incomparable. More significantly, however, it is important because in its brilliance, it demonstrates the need for studies that focus more directly on the quality of life among a particular people, living in a particular neighborhood— studies that consider the consequences of industrial expansion and contraction.

This book is a study of a set of symbiotic relationships: relationships involving owners, managers, and workers engaged in the manufacture of the Model T. It directly involves the Crystal Palace and its neighborhood, Highland Park, Michigan, and somewhat less directly it involves the city of Detroit. My primary focus is on the wage-earner and the underclass living in the shadows of the Crystal Palace. Secondarily I give consideration to the quality of life experienced by the Model T cohort of Ford workers. In short, by focusing on the Model T cohort of Ford workers (1910-1927), I hope to show how the expansion and contraction of operations in the Crystal Palace affected the quality of life in its neighborhood and in adjacent communities.

Even though Highland Park, a city within the city limits of Detroit, was the town that built the Model T, the birthplace of the modern assembly line, and the first city that clearly owed its existence to the automotive industry, relatively little scholarly attention has been devoted to the social and cultural history of this small but extraordinarily important enclave. With the exception of Ellen Hathaway's two books, *The History of Highland Park*, which was written for children, and *From Wilderness to City*, along with the paragraph or two in prominent works such as Allan Nevins and Zunz's, there are no published studies focusing directly on the history of Highland Park. Given the virtual absence of published work on this important community, this book begins to fill a void in our understanding of the historic relationship between the Ford Motor Company's Crystal Palace and Highland Park, and in our knowledge of how that relationship affected the quality of life among assembly line workers, their families, and their neighborhoods in the period from 1910 to 1927.

My analysis of the relationship of the expansion and contraction of the Ford Motor Company in Highland Park and on the resulting impact on the quality of life in the region. Chapter 1, "Highland Park Before the Crystal Palace: The Genesis of a Midwestern Island Community," provides some insight into what the community was like before the coming of the Crystal Palace and the Model T; here, a special effort is made to identify the movers and shakers and to show how they helped to shape the economic life of the community and to lay the foundation for its transformation. Chapter 2, "Frederick Winslow Taylor and Scientific Management," discusses the union of Taylorism and Fordism and traces the main features in the evolution of the Crystal Palace from about 1910 to 1914. This chapter shows how rapid advances in machine-tool technology laid the foundation for the "logical next step," the moving assembly line, with the need for labor resulting in an unprecedented and explosive change in the size and composition of the community. Chapter 3, "Technological Innovation and the Demographic Transformation of Highland Park," outlines the major population and demographic changes resulting from the demands of the new, revolutionary system of production, and analyzes these changes as part of a larger trend. Chapter 4, "White- and Blue-Collar Workers in the Crystal Palace: Building the Model T and Forging the New Social Order," examines the new pattern of stratification in the plant and discusses how the principles of scientific management contributed to the development of a new manager-class.

Chapter 5, "From Ethnic Squalor to White-Collar Splendor: Some Observations on the Quality of Life of the Model T Cohort, 1910-1927," contrasts housing conditions found in densely populated neighborhoods near the Highland Park plant with those found in other areas of Detroit and suggests that the physical differences in these communities closely approximate the social and psychological distances observed in the workplace. Chapter 6, "Ford's Welfare Work: Americanization and the Molding of the Ford Man," is an assessment of the impact of Ford's profit-sharing plan and its effect on Ford workers, with emphasis on understanding the work of Ford's Sociological Department and its effectiveness in improving the quality of life of the "ethnics" who labored in the Crystal Palace production plant. Chapter 7, "Ford Men Living In: Boarding and Boarders in Highland Park and Vicinity, 1910-1927," is a discussion of home and housing conditions in Highland Park and vicinity and Ford's efforts to improve them. Finally, the Conclusion notes of some of the most important findings, discusses some of the most significant data problems, and considers one direction that future research might take.

In addition to the focus on the wage-earner and the Model T cohort, I hope to identify a strategy and sources of data which will permit the longitudinal analysis of quality of life issues, and with a little luck, to ignite further study of the Crystal Palace and its place in shaping the social and cultural history of Highland Park.

1

Highland Park Before the Crystal Palace: The Genesis of a Midwestern Island Community

Highland Park, first known as Woodwardville, and later Whitewood before becoming the City of Highland Park in 1889, was carved out of a virtual wilderness where the life cycle was determined by the seasons. Wild animals such as deer, bear, turkeys, honey bees, and mosquitoes were plentiful.[1] A variety of trees thrived in the area; pine, elm, and oak trees dotted the landscape, but the whitewood tree was especially prominent. In the spring, the fragrance of flowering fruit trees and berry bushes mingled with the scents of wild animals in various stages of their reproductive cycles, the barnyard manures, and the heavy springtime odor of hogs. Summer harvests gave way to the cool breezes of fall, which carried ducks, geese and other fowl in their southward migration. The brilliant reds, oranges, and yellows of trees painted first the horizon and then the landscape. Cold, deep white winters slowed the pace of human and animal life, as the cycle started anew.[2]

This erstwhile wilderness was located about six miles northeast of downtown Detroit in what was once Greenfield Township, and today lies entirely within the city limits of Detroit. Trapezoidal in shape and about 647 feet above sea level, Highland Park's 2.98 square miles are bisected by Woodward Avenue; McNichols Road (formerly Six Mile Road), which marks the northern boundary, while Tuxedo Avenue on the west side of Woodward and Tennyson Avenue on the east side of Woodward mark the southern boundary; the Grand Trunk Railroad right-of-way and Thompson Avenue serve, respectively, as the eastern and western boundaries.[3] It was as a result of an accident that this wilderness was opened to settlement.

The entire city of Detroit was destroyed by fire in 1805; in order that a new court house and jail could be built, the federal government gave the city of Detroit permission to sell land north of Grand Boulevard, including the swamp land where Highland

Map 1.1

Highland Park & Hamtramck
Within the city limits of Detroit, Michigan

Michigan

Detroit

CANADA

River Rouge

Highland
Park

Hamtramck

Detroit River

Dearborn

0   5 Miles

City Limits 1920

Map 1.2

The City of Highland Park c. 1915
Located within the City of Detroit, Wayne County, Michigan
Approximate Scale 1" = 1200'

Ford Motor Company

Detroit Railroad

Hamtramck

Park would eventually be built. Thus, it was an indirect result of the 1805 fire that the federally owned land was publicly sold.

In 1818 the highland which was separated from Detroit by a swamp, was purchased by Judge Augustus B. Woodward, but owing to the obstacles presented by the swamp, his attempts to found a village were unsuccessful. The swamp was also the major obstacle for B.F.H. Withersell, another Detroit judge who attempted to establish a village in 1836.[4] Although there were settlers, the area would not achieve the status of a village until Capt. William H. Stevens' efforts had attracted enough financial backing to eliminate the swamp.

Most of the early settlers were New England Protestants. The first known settler was Richard Ford (apparently not related to the Henry Ford family), a farmer of English descent arrived about 1818. Ford built his cabin on a ridge that was separated from Detroit by the swamp; the ridge (i.e., the highland) has since been leveled, but it was the geographic feature for which the village was named. The Fords were farmers who tilled the soil with wooden plows, and who lost crops to flooding lowlands, bear, deer, and wild turkeys. Richard Ford's son, George Thomas Ford, was born c. 1843 in Greenfield Township, and later operated a prosperous wholesale business.

The Riley, Tyler, and Pallister families were also among the early settlers. Richard Riley, a native of Yorkshire, England, arrived in the United States in 1830, bringing a wife and three children to settle in Greenfield Township. Mary Riley Maskill, one of the three children stated, "I came to Detroit with my parents in 1831. We settled on land near Greenfield. It was a dismal wilderness then, with great forests filled with Indians."[5] The Riley family apparently owned land on both sides of English Settlement Road, later renamed Glendale Avenue. Howell S. Tyler came in an ox-cart from Vermont, arriving on March 17, 1849.[6] The Howell farm extended from the alley north of Waverly to Monterey, and from Waverly and Hamilton. Having taken eight weeks to sail from England to America, William, Robert, and George Pallister arrived in 1846; Robert took up farming on the land located at Woodward and Pallister Avenues. Ten years later, three more brothers, Paul, Thomas, and Joseph arrived in Detroit and walked to Robert's farm. Paul and Thomas took up farming in Hamtramck.[7]

Several families in the second cohort of Highland Park settlers, most notably the Langdon, Mott, and Fitzgerald families, were distinguished through providing soldiers for the Union army during the Civil War. John Langdon had come to America in 1830 when he was two years old; upon the death of his father, John became the ward of his uncle, Jared Davison, who was then living in Highland Park. As a young man, John Langdon bought a twenty-acre farm on Woodward Avenue. In 1862, John Langdon enlisted in the 24th Michigan Infantry.

John T. Mott was born on April 4, 1846 in Franklin, Connecticut, and later moved to Port Huron, Michigan, with his parents. John was among the first volunteers to come forward for the Union cause during the Civil War; he joined Company E of the 16th Michigan Infantry on August 13, 1861. During the war, John Mott was cited for bravery and promoted to second lieutenant; after approximately three years of service, he was discharged from Company C of the 16th Michigan Infantry on May 12, 1863. After the war, John (affectionately known as Uncle John) opened a general store at the southeast corner of Woodward and Davison. John Mott married into one of the original families of Highland Park; on March 19, 1874, he wed Emily A. Davison, and both the marriage and the store prospered. Even though Adolphus Thombley was already operating a post office in his home in 1873, Mott opened the Whitewood post office (the name of the community had not yet been changed to Highland Park) in his store in 1876.[8] Unlike Langdon and Mott, who served as Michigan volunteers, Fitzgerald joined the Union forces before moving to Michigan.

James D. Fitzgerald was born in Castle Gregory, Ireland, on March 30, 1825. In 1841, Fitzgerald arrived in the United States, settling in Vermont in the fall of that year. The following year he moved to Cleveland, and then to Beria, Ohio, where he worked in stone quarries. Fitzgerald's wife-to-be, Mary C. Runion, had been born in Prescott, Canada, on January 20, 1835. The wedding took place in 1850, and in due time four children were born: Mary A., who would become Mrs. William Davison; and Ella, followed by Jennie N., who would become Mrs. George Pell; and finally, James Fitzgerald, the only son produced by the marriage. Having enlisted in Company E of the 65th Regiment of the Ohio Volunteers, Fitzgerald was wounded and subsequently given a disability discharge. It was not until 1864 that the Fitzgerald family moved to Michigan, initially settling in Detroit on Woodward Avenue, but within a year purchasing a thirty-acre farm in Highland Park. In addition to his farm work, Fitzgerald worked as a landscape gardener for Senator Thomas Palmer. Fitzgerald, known throughout the community for his kindness, died in July of 1883, and his wife, the former Mary C. Runion, died on June 2, 1917.[9]

To the extent that the Langdon, Mott, and Fitzgerald families intermarried with first generation settlers, and were principally farmers, they were typical Highland Parkers. They were Protestant farmers, seemingly in agreement about issues of mutual concern. It appears that most of the farms were approximately twenty acres, but there were several thirty-acre farms, and it is conceivable that some were larger. Thomas V. Brown was able to purchase a Gaar Scott threshing engine in 1890, and threshed grain throughout the region for twenty-six years; he recalled threshing for the Davisons, Tylers, Pallisters, and Fords in Highland Park. Brown also recalled that during one harvesting season, he threshed oats for a whole week on Senator Palmer's farm at Six Mile and Woodward Avenue.

Stonehouse, his wife, and daughter, Isobel, left England for America in 1851. After traveling for seven weeks, the Stonehouses landed in Detroit at the southern end of Pontiac Plank Road, where they were met by George's brothers. Isobel recalled that the spring of that year included the considerably hard work of clearing land before planting crops. The land between the tree stumps was sown with grain, small patches of potatoes and corn. Mrs. Stonehouse did her marketing in Detroit, where she bartered berries and farm produce for staples such as sugar, flour, and salt. George did the work of a veterinary, and like other farmers (all of whom apparently had one or more hunting dogs), hunted for deer, bear, and other wild game. Considered together, life as experienced by the Stonehouse, Langdon, Mott, and Fitzgerald families was typical for the second cohort of those who settled in Highland Park.

Except for adding their numbers to the population, the second cohort of settlers did not live much differently than those who had preceded them. It was the third wave of settlers, the real movers and shakers coming in the latter decades of the nineteenth century, who would begin significant diversification of the culture of Highland Park. For example, the first factory, the McAlpine shoe factory, was established in 1891.[10] It was located on the north corner of Woodward and Colorado Avenues in the old waterworks building owned by Captain Stevens. In addition to the McAlpine shoe factory, the Seiss wagon factory and Percheon's backsmith shop were prominent among the non-farm economic activities in late nineteenth century Highland Park. In other words, it was the third generation, including Stevens who would be the most influential among them, Voorhis, Siess, Smith, et al. whose non-farm interests would begin the spiral of significant changes in the culture of Highland Park.

Robert Smith came to Highland Park around 1900, and he is representative of residents who would live with one foot in the past, and the other in the twentieth century. While working at the Union Market on Cadillac Square, he met George Ford, who often sold calves and hogs in the market. Ford invited Smith to visit his farm located at Ford and Woodward Avenues in Highland Park; apparently Smith was favorably impressed, and purchased a lot on the corner of John R and Stevens Avenue where, at a cost of about $350.00, he built a farmhouse with dimensions of eighteen by twenty-four feet. Reminiscing about life on the farm, Smith related that he bought a prize Jersey cow, formerly owned by Senator Palmer, from Joe Marshall. Consequently, he had to wake up at four in the morning, and before leaving for the market located in downtown Detroit, he had to milk the cow, and feed the chickens, which roosted under the house until he was able to build a chicken coop. To get to the market, he rode his bicycle as far as Holznagle's, the local florist shop, and rode the street car from there. Smith also recalled that in order to cook or wash, he had to carry water from the neighbors; on Saturdays he took his weekly bath in a wash tub behind the stove. It appears that Smith was highly regarded by many people in the community. In 1912 he was elected village treasurer, in which capacity he served for twenty-seven years, while being opposed by no more than three candidates for that office.[11]

Siess and Voorhis were among the third generation of settlers whose primary activities consisted of non-agricultural work. Charles August Siess was the village wagon-maker and blacksmith. In 1882 Siess leased four acres from Stevens and moved his family from his mother-in-law's farm on Holbrook Avenue and Russell Street, to a little house near his shop. During the economic difficulties of 1893, which affected the entire nation, Siess went out of business, but the family continued to live in the area and some of them would work in the Crystal Palace.

George Voorhis, who would become the village assessor in 1913, came to Highland Park around 1895 with his father and mother, and three younger children, Fred, Alice, and Dora. Voorhis had come to Highland Park as the proprietor and manager of the Highland Park Resort Hotel, which included the race-track leased from Capt. William Stevens. The resort was situated on fifty-eight acres, with Oakland and Woodward Avenues as the east and west boundaries, respectively, and Manchester as the south boundary.

The main attractions of the resort were harness racing and a well producing mineral water used for medicinal purposes. Voorhis leased the track to the Highland Park Jockey Club, which brought in professional drivers and horses for much of the year, but especially during the racing season, from June to September. The hotel had fifteen rooms and was usually filled to capacity; often reserved for owners of horses, their families, and jockeys. George Voorhis reported that according to City Hall records, in 1895 a tax totaling $164.00 was levied against the fifty-eight acres where the hotel was located, and the personal property of the Highland Park Jockey Club was assessed at $33,000.00.[12] This hotel and race track, for the moment owned and operated by the Voorhis family, would later be sold to the Ford Motor Company and become the site of the Crystal Palace.

The one-eyed Capt. William H. Stevens stands out as the most prominent personage in Highland Park's early development. Stevens was born in New York State in 1819, and moved to Wisconsin, and then to Michigan while he was still a youngster. In Michigan, he became acquainted with some men employed by the Summit Mining Company (this company was apparently based in Boston, Massachusetts); Stevens managed to get himself hired by the company as an "official land looker," or prospector in the copper regions of Michigan. Taking valuable lessons he had learned while working for the Summit Mining Company, Stevens went to Colorado to seek his own fortune in mining. After making a considerable fortune in silver mining in Colorado, he returned to Michigan in 1887 and began a vigorous effort to develop the swamplands north of the city of Detroit. Stevens was able to attract the support of Senator Thomas W. Palmer in his project to develop the highlands. In addition to lending his name to Stevens's efforts, Senator Palmer donated one hundred acres of his Log Cabin Farm to be used as a Detroit Park; located north of the highland, the one hundred acres donated by Senator Palmer were low and wet, and sewers were dug to drain the park site. Since the park had been donated as a city park, public funds were used to pay for drainage sewers. Apparently to no one's surprise, the drainage sewers provided drainage to the swamps between the highland and the Detroit River. Previously known as Wood-wardville and Whitewood, the village of Highland Park, with about 400 inhabitants, was officially etched into Greenfield Township in 1889.[13]

More than any other individual in the third generation of citizens, Captain Stevens had his hand in shaping daily life in Highland Park. Stevens helped to lay out the streets, and loaned money to people so that they could build their homes. Stevens also played an important role in bringing the streetcar to the village in 1886. Improved versions of the streetcar ran on Woodward for nearly seventy years (1886-1956), and it was the last line to run in Michigan. In 1892 Highland Avenue was the first street to be graded, and in 1909 the world's first mile of concrete road was laid on Woodward Avenue between Six Mile and Seven Mile Roads. While Stevens, a real mover and shaker, was instrumental in developing the infrastructure of the community, he also showed a special interest in schools.

The first village schools were the direct result of Stevens's efforts. In 1892 the second floor of the waterworks building, located on the corner of Colorado and Woodward, and owned by Stevens, became a schoolhouse. Stevens bought furnishings and supplies for the school, and that fall hired Edna Phelps to teach the class of sixteen children. The next year, Clifton Gordon was hired to teach the older children in the same room where Edna Phelps continued to instruct the younger children. Sometime during the year, the school was moved to a store on the corner of McClean and Woodward Avenues. The first building to be especially constructed as a school was a four-room structure located on the south side of East Buena Vista near Woodward; known as the Stevens School, it opened with an enrollment of seventy-five pupils. Soon after the completion of the Stevens School, Robert Barber arrived in Highland Park to become the village's first superintendent of schools.[14]

Having exerted a great deal of energy and influence and financial resources to building the village of Highland Park, at 82 years of age Stevens died in 1901 in his farm home at the present site of the McGregor Library. Stevens's civic influence continued to be felt when, after his death, the daughter of his close friend, David Whitney, bought the Stevens house and used it as a home for crippled and homeless children. Later the children's home was given to the City of Highland Park for use as a library, and in 1926 the stone house was replaced by the impressive structure that now houses the McGregor Library. Currently, the McGregor Library is the only known repository of Highland Park's first newspaper, the *Highland Park Times*, which began publication in 1909. In 1917 another weekly paper, the *Highland Park News*, was published by Arthur Kingsley. After a period of military service, Kingsley returned to Highland Park and purchased the *Highland Park Times*, which he combined with the *Highland Park News* to found the *Highland Parker*, which was published until 1926. It is appropriate that some issues of these newspapers have been deposited at the site that Capt. William H. Stevens called home.

Coincidentally, Stevens's death was a harbinger of a new era in Highland Park. Throughout the lives of the first two generations of settlers, and for much of the lifetime of the third generation, Highland Park was typical of midwestern "island communities" such as those studied by Robert H. Wiebe.[15] Wiebe has suggested that in the late nineteenth century, America was essentially a "nation of loosely connected island communities," villages and small towns much like Highland Park. Wiebe began his analysis by noting that the purpose of his study was to describe the breakdown of island communities and the emergence of a new system. He characterized island communities as satellites of larger towns, cities and metropolises, to which they looked for "markets and supplies, credit and news." Thus, Highland Park is seen as a satellite of Detroit. Wiebe observed that life in the island communities was regulated by the rhythms of agriculture: "the pace of the sun's day, the working and watching of the crop months, the cycle of the seasons."[16] In the same sense as the growth and harvest cycles of fruits, vegetables and grains, as well as the cycles of wild and domesticated animals, human society and social life were also predictable.

Island communities such as Highland Park were remarkably stable with little evidence of internal conflict. As Wiebe expressed it, these communities were "usually homogeneous, usually Protestant: communities enjoying an inner stability which the coming and going of members did not disturb. Moreover, even when new towns and villages were established in other locations, continuity and stability were undisturbed because the gathering families brought the same familiar habits and customs."[17] The homogeneity of these communities, apparently, contributed to the lack of significant open conflict.

From a distance the towns and villages characterized as island communities appeared to be egalitarian democracies, "sustaining neither an aristocracy of name nor an aristocracy of occupation." But despite appearances and the lack of conflict, "each community was divided by innumerable, fine gradations." At the top sat a few men who not only had greater wealth than their neighbors, but who, owing primarily to their contacts outside the community, controlled access to potential wealth. These men—merchants, bankers, successful farmers, and the like—were referred to as "mister" (or "captain" in the case of Stevens in Highland Park), not "Bill" or "Sam."[18] Although differences in religion, language, and skin color distinguished individuals, groups, and even entire communities from each other, generally speaking, the island communities such as Highland Park were ethnically, culturally, and religiously homogenous societies without overt, socially important conflict. Before January 1, 1910, when the first Model T Ford was built in the Crystal Palace, Highland Park was a typical island community, but that was about to change.

Of the many changes wrought in Highland Park by the pyramid of technological innovation, employment, production, and the social policies emanating from the Crystal Palace, a few had an enormous impact of the social order and quality of life experienced in the community. If the quality of life is defined as "a function of the objective conditions and subjective attitudes involving a defined area of concern," and measured by social, economic, political, health and environmental indicators, then it is clear that the quality of life experienced by the third and fourth cohorts of those inhabiting Highland Park and its vicinity was radically different from that of their predecessors; moreover, it is clear that most of the difference may be directly attributable to the influence of the Ford Motor Company.[19]

2

Frederick Winslow Taylor
and Scientific Management

The 1914 Model T, even by standards of that time, was ugly. It had a 56-inch gauge and a 100-inch wheel base, wood spoke wheels, and half elliptic springs in both the front and rear. The chassis was supported the same, front and rear, at the middle of the end cross members. The distinctive feature of this design was the triangular bracing of both the front and rear axles with a globe-joint triangle attachment to the chassis frame. This design gave an absolutely free vertical wheel position and adjustment to each of the four wheels independently, therefore allowing adjustments to suit road surface and level variations. This automobile was powered by a four-cylinder, four-cycle, water cooled engine with three and three-quarter-inch pistons, a four-inch stroke, and had a 20 horsepower rating. It had a planetary transmission (with two forward speeds and a reverse) that was coupled by one universal joint to the drive-shaft, and by means of a bevel gear and a balance gear, connected to the rear axles. On good roads it could reach 35 to 40 miles per hour, and could go a distance of 18 to 20 miles per gallon of gasoline.[1] By 1914, the closely coordinated labor of more than 570 white-collar employees, a large number of factory "executives," and about 1,600 blue-collar workers, all of whom were indirectly under the influence of Frederick Winslow Taylor, were able to build an average of 1,000 Model Ts per day.[2]

Before turning to a consideration of the technological and managerial revolution that gave birth to the Model T, it is important to place Taylor's work in the proper perspective. The emergence of management engineering, or "scientific management" as it was popularly known, can be associated with the enormous increase in the size and complexity of American corporations between the Civil War and about 1900.[3] In a manner similar to that in the professions of medicine, real estate, and education, which became increasingly more specialized and segmented in response to the demands and opportunities offered by a rapidly growing and increasingly complex industrial society, engineers recognized an opportunity to create a new specialization within the profession of industrial engineering. However, unlike other established professions, scientific management carried relatively little traditional (intellectual) baggage.[4] More precisely, it may be noted that the origin of modern personnel management is to be found in "two converging strands in American economic life. One is the movement which has been designated 'welfare work.' The other, associated with the profession of engineering, is Scientific Management."[5]

At the outset, "efficiency" was the primary concern of engineers who became associated with the development of the new profession that became known as management engineering. Their traditional concerns had been with material, structure, and machine process, but in the midst of revolutionary developments in corporate organization and in machine and tool technology, it soon became apparent that greater "efficiency" could only be achieved when the workman was taken into consideration. This new direction taken by some engineers around the beginning of the twentieth century is often associated with the name Frederick Winslow Taylor, the most famous of the engineers and the recognized father of scientific management. Students who search the literature of American management will find abundant evidence that the "aims, principles and procedures first presented by Taylor have, like the ripples of a stone cast into a pool, spread out into American industry, although many a management of 1919 [and beyond] may not know the source of that which it believes and practices."[6]

Among the critical steps towards the insertion of mechanical engineers into the "management engineering" mold, the first was taken with the founding of the American Society of Mechanical Engineers (A.S.M.E.) in 1880. It should be noted that a variety of specialties, such as accounting and marketing, had already developed within corporate structures. "There is [however] no such evidence of early application of the principles of specialization to labor administration. Before 1900, the day-to-day relations with labor were in the hands of foremen."[7]

By 1886 a new direction was made apparent. At the annual meeting of A.S.M.E. in Chicago on May 26, the first in a long series of papers on management was presented to the members. Two of the papers, "The Shop Order System of Accounts" by

Capt. Henry Metcalfe, and "Inventory Valuation of Machinery Plant" by Oberlin Smith, had no lasting impact on the development of "management engineering." But the third, by Henry Townsend, "The Engineer as An Economist," in which the presenter reminded his listeners that the engineer's value to any firm was ultimately measured in dollars and cents, stands out as a watershed in industrial management. The discussion following the presentation of these three papers was lively, and one of the persons involved was Frederick Winslow Taylor, a thirty-five-year-old engineer who had joined A.S.M.E. in 1885. Here, in 1886 is where Taylor began his contribution to management engineering, although his first formal presentation to the society would not come until 1895.

Four years after Frederick A. Halsey delivered a paper in which he introduced the element of "time," as a consideration in devising incentive pay,[8] Taylor presented his first paper to A.S.M.E. Taylor had a long-standing interest in the "time element," and his presentation, "A Piece Rate System, Being a Step Toward Partial Solution of the Labor Problem,"[9] was an analysis of this potentially vital element. For the next several years, thinking among engineers continued to focus primarily on using wages as a means of achieving efficiency on the part of workers. It was Taylor's opinion that "the greatest obstacle to efficient production was poor management, simply because employers knew little about the elements of production."[10] In other words, Taylor believed that the emphasis on wage incentives as a means of achieving efficiency in production was wrong-headed. Therefore, Taylor offered a remedy for the misdirection of attention during the 1903 meeting of A.S.M.E. in Saratoga, New York. There he read his famous Paper Number 1003 bearing the title, "Shop Management"[11] and in which he outlined the principles through which, he argued, management could unite high wages with low labor costs.[12] As in the case of the "Piece Rate" paper, the "Shop Management" paper "failed to stimulate sympathetic interest in the idea that a day's work could be measured,"[13] and thereby used as the foundation for achieving efficiency in production. It was not until eight years later that the Eastern Rate Case hearings of 1910-1911 gave Taylor's ideas a sudden currency under the name of scientific management.[14]

Prior to 1910 Taylor was known only in American engineering and industrial circles, but as a direct result of Interstate Commerce Commission hearings conducted in 1910 Taylor quickly

became an international celebrity. The ICC was established to pro-
tect the public interest, and had the authority to conduct hearings
on railroad rate increases. According to one perspective, the ICC
served the public interest by keeping rail rates low, and if railroad
revenues were already lower than costs, the solution was more
careful management and greater productivity. In the political cli-
mate of the period, more careful management was the popularly
supported solution and it was the policy emphasized by the ICC
between 1906 and 1917.[15] Louis Brandeis, as an attorney in the
eastern railroad rate hearings and future Supreme Court justice,
argued that the railroads did not need the increase. Rather, argued
Brandeis, what the railroads needed "was a dose of scientific
management, Frederick Winslow Taylor's system of science-bred
industrial efficiency."[16] In making this argument, Louis Brandeis
made Taylor a national icon.

Innovations in the Crystal Palace and the popularization of
the principles of scientific management occurred simultaneously.
Ford engineers were evidently aware of Taylor's work, and as evident in Flander's improved tooling system at the Piquette plant,
in Hawkins' departmentalization, and P.E. Martin's elementary
time studies, they had undoubtedly absorbed some of Taylor's
ideas.[17] Among managers in the Crystal Palace, Clarence W. Avery
had the broadest grasp of scientific management. "He had read
widely, knew the latest European and American advances in engineering, and kept in touch with the ideas of men like" Taylor.[18]
And, as Allan Nevins noted, the year (1911) that the Crystal
Palace was in full use, "was the year in which Taylor published
The Principles of Scientific Management, and laid before Congress
his report on the Taylor system." Moreover, Taylor himself recognized the independent implementation of the principles of which
he is the recognized articulator.

According to the record as reported by Nevins, Taylor lec-
tured to Detroit area engineers and managers on at least two separate occasions. In 1909 Taylor had spoken for more than four
hours at the Packard plant, and late in 1910 he addressed a group
consisting of more than six hundred superintendents and foremen
employed in Detroit area industries. On the latter occasion, Taylor
was told that "without special prompting or counsel," several
Detroit area firms "had anticipated his ideas." Having been
informed of this development, Taylor expressed his interest and
stated that it was the "first instance in which a group of manufacturers had undertaken to install the principles of scientific man-

agement without the aid of experts."[20] Clearly, then, independent of Taylor's writings, the machine process in the automotive industry, most thoroughly in the Crystal Palace, was generating and perfecting its own procedures. It is significant that "plant engineers and production superintendents, knowing little theory but schooled in the machine shop, foundry, and assembly room . . . were creating a system of management to meet" their practical problems. As Nevins has stated, "Ford, Wills, Galamb, Emde, and Sorensen may well have learned something from Taylor, but they could also have taught him something."[21] Whatever the role played by Taylor's scientific management, the revolution in the Crystal Palace would soon be consolidated.

Whether or not the system instituted in the Crystal Palace was drawn directly from Taylor's work, it was clearly in line with his prescriptions, and therefore, the principles outlined by Taylor offer an excellent framework within which to analyze the process and the results of Ford's managerial revolution. Recognized as the "father of scientific management," and the "original efficiency expert," Taylor had begun careful time and motion studies in the machine shop of the Midvale Steel Company in 1881,[22] and in 1893 in Philadelphia he opened an office where he worked as a consultant in shop management and manufacturing costs.[23] In describing his book (*Shop Management*), Taylor wrote, "This book is written mainly with the object of advocating high wages and low labor cost as the foundation of the best management, of pointing out general principles which render it possible to maintain these conditions even under the most trying circumstances, and of indicating the various steps which the writer thinks should be taken in changing from a poor system to a better type of management."[24] Taylor maintained that scientific management, "in its essence, consists of a certain philosophy, which results, in a combination of four great underlying principles of management." In brief, the four principles included the development of a true science; the scientific selection of the workman; his scientific education and development; and intimate, friendly cooperation between the management and the men.[25]

It may be argued that in the Crystal Palace, the first, second, and third principles of scientific management were accomplished simultaneously. Taylor explained the four underlying principles of management in his 1912 testimony to the House of Representatives Special Committee. Taylor stated that the first principle involved managers in the deliberate collection of "the great mass of traditional knowledge which in the past has been in the heads of workmen." This "first principle may be called the development of a science to replace the old rule-of-thumb knowledge workmen had . . . and of which there was no permanent record."[26] The second principle, Taylor continued, "is the scientific selection and the progressive development of the workingmen"; and "the third of the principles of scientific management is bringing the scientifically selected and trained workmen together."[27] Certainly, the Ford workmen were not "scientifically selected," and therefore, the second and third principles were not accomplished according to Taylor's prescription. The objectives were achieved through the scientific selection and progressive development of tools and machines, rather than through the scientific selection of workmen. In other words, in the initial stages of the production of the Model T, the conditions that Taylor's second and third principles were expected to satisfy were created primarily through the use of tools and the arrangement of machines, rather than by the scientific selection and education of workmen.

The fourth principle, Taylor continued in his testimony, "is perhaps the most difficult of the four principles of scientific management for the average man to understand."[28] Worded somewhat differently in *Shop Management,* the fourth principle calls for an almost equal division of the actual work of the company between workmen and management. "That is, the work which under the old type of management practically all was done by the workmen, under the new [system] is divided into two great divisions [classes], and one of these divisions is deliberately handed over to those on the management side."[29] In the Crystal Palace, the successful implementation of the principles of scientific management was marked by the emergence (late in 1914) of mass-produced Model Ts from the continuous production assembly lines.

The seeds for the Model T, and its handmaiden, the first mass-production automated assembly line, were sown with Henry Ford's early "tinkering" with automotive contraptions, and with his "entrepreneurial" adventures. What would become the Model T, recognizable throughout the entire world, first appeared in the Ford plant at Piquette and Beaubien Streets, but would not be fully developed until the move to the Crystal Palace in Highland Park. In the process of developing and refining the world's most popular driving machine, Henry Ford (sometimes directly, and often indirectly) was involved in the origination of a number of revolutionary innovations in automotive engineering, machine-tool technology, labor management, and marketing that literally changed where and how Americans would live.

Born July 30, 1863, on a farm in Dearborn, Michigan, Henry Ford was destined to play a leading role in revolutionizing automotive production. While he was a youngster living in Dearborn, Ford often worked as a water boy for farmers in the village of Whitewood, which would later become the city of Highland Park. The task of a water boy was to keep the tanks of steam-driven threshers filled. At the age of sixteen, spurred on by interests in mechanical operations, Ford left Dearborn and moved to Detroit, where he worked as a machinist's apprentice in a shop that was building marine engines for vessels employed in the lake traffic. Within a few years young Henry Ford had achieved the status of journeyman, and he was hired to travel along the waterfront and to the larger farms where he installed and repaired steam and gasoline engines.[30] In subsequent years Ford became the chief engineer (i.e., machine operator) at the Edison Illuminating Company, which later became Detroit Edison.

In 1896, during his employment at Edison, Ford built his quadricycle. Except for the axles, wheels, and steering rod, the quadricycle tested during the early morning hours of June 4, 1896, had a 49-inch wheel base, was mostly wood and weighed about 500 pounds. It was powered by a three- to four-horsepower engine with two cylinders, two and one-half-inch bore and a six-inch stroke. The motor had a flywheel that was spun in neutral to start and a two-speed transmission was connected to the wheels by a drive belt.

Following a few years of experiments with the quadricycle, Ford attracted the financial support of local businessmen, and in 1899 the Detroit Automobile Company was formed with Henry Ford as the mechanical superintendent. Owing primarily to Ford's doubts about the adequacy of the horseless carriage produced by the Detroit Automobile Company (August 15, 1899, to February 1, 1901), and perhaps due to his interest in racing, the company was dissolved.[31]

Evidently, Ford had observed a correlation between winning races, technological improvements, and increased sales[32] and was now convinced that the builder of a winning race car would attract financial backing; therefore, in the spring of 1901 he turned to racing, the greatest and most public way to show which automobile was best.[33] Along with Childe Harold Wills (C.H. Wills), Ford built a race car with two horizontally opposed cylinders with seven inches bore and stroke.[34] The Ford-Wills vehicle entered and won a race against Alexander Winton of Cleveland, Ohio, at the Detroit Race Club in Grosse Pointe, Michigan, on October 10, 1901. For winning this twenty-five-mile race, Ford won $1,000 and an ornamental cut-glass bowl; but, "the fame, the money and the cut-glass bowl were not the only important results of that October day . . . Ford and Oldfield had their first meeting that afternoon."[35] The notoriety and prestige resulting from this impressive victory evidently increased confidence in Ford, and by the end of November the Henry Ford Company was established with the backing of Clarence Black, Lem Brown, Mark Hopkins, William Murphy, and Albert White.

Rather than getting on with the finalization of "the automobile for every person" Ford continued working on race cars, and eventually produced the famed "999" and the "Arrow."[36] Apparently, in a spate of mutual dissatisfaction, Ford left the company on March 10, 1902, and concentrated on building race cars, while the company was renamed and reorganized to produce Henry Leland's Cadillacs. With the financial backing of a race driver named Tom Cooper, Ford, Wills, Ed ("Spider") Huff, Oliver Bartels et al. continued to work on the two race cars which were completed by the summer in time for a well-publicized race scheduled for October 15, 1902. Cooper brought in Barney Oldfield, "a real race driver," who won the race by over a lap in the five-mile event and in the process set a new American record of 5:28.

With this victory Ford became relatively famous and was quickly recognized as a "good investment." Ford and Alexander Malcolmson, one of the largest coal dealers in Detroit, had already drawn up a partnership agreement in the law offices of Horace H. Rackham and John W. Anderson. But the success of the "999" had apparently added fire to the enthusiasm of Malcolmson, who not only made money a bit more available to Ford but also formed with Ford a business under the name of Ford and Malcolmson Ltd.[37]

In the winter of 1902 Ford toyed with the idea of becoming a race car promoter. Henri Fournier, the famous French driver of the time, had just set a record on New York's Coney Island Boulevard on November 16. His mark for the mile was 69.5 miles per hour and Ford thought he could build a car to run against Fournier's, and they could barnstorm around the country. A letter to his brother said: "If I can bring Mr. Fournier onto line there is a barrel of money in this business. It was his proposition and I don't see why he won't fall in line. If he don't I will challenge him untill [sic] I am black in the face." The letter continued, "my company will kick about me following racing but they will get advertising and I expect to make $ where I can't make a cent at manufacturing."[38] Ford finally left the Henry Ford Company in March 1902 to go racing.

And race he did. So much so, that on June 23, 1909, he won a the highly publicized transcontinental race from New York to Seattle. With this victory "the advertising drums started to beat," and the classic hard-sell ads of the time boasted: "A duplicate of the winner with a five-passenger touring car body costs you $850. No other car was entered that costs less than five times as much. The winner was a stock car. Any Model T could do as well. It's the one reliable car that does not require a $10,000 income to buy, a $5,000 bank account to run and a college course in engineering to keep in order. Better get in line if you want August delivery."[39]

By his racing success, Ford had shown the potential value of using automobile racing to advertise a particular car. Now armed with an ever increasing supply of knowledge about the mechanics of automotive vehicles, Ford resumed work on a two-cylinder passenger car, and he persuaded a new group of investors to join him in forming the Ford Motor Company in 1903. The newly organized Ford Motor Company produced over a thousand cars in its first year. In 1904 and for several years thereafter, the Ford Motor Company introduced a succession of new models, including the four-cylinder Model N during 1906-1907. The Model N proved to be an able competitor against the much more expensive cars of the period and was the first sustained attempt to build and market an inexpensive vehicle that was not a horseless-buggy. Between 1903 and 1905 the Ford Motor Company was among the top four American producers of automotive vehicles; in 1906 Ford became No. 1.

Ford's rapid ascent to the No. 1 position among automotive manufacturers was assured when the plant on the corner of Piquette and Beaubien Streets was streamlined in 1904-1905. The changes included dividing certain tasks into simple operations that less-skilled workers could perform. Under the new arrangement, workers pushed huge bins of parts up and down the rows of stationary cars, with each gang stopping to install a particular part such as a fender, wheels, the dashboard, etc., before moving to the next car.[40] As a result of the changes introduced in the plant at Piquette and Beaubien Streets, production increased considerably; however, the increase was not rapid enough, especially after the successful introduction of the Model T in 1908, to keep up with demand.

When the Model T made its debut, Ford's assembly techniques had remained virtually unchanged during the five years since he began work in Strelow's carpenter shop. With the soaring demand for the Model T, it became apparent that, even though the Ford plant at Piquette and Beaubien was only three years old, it was already out of date. Highland Park was the location chosen for the new facility to become known as the Crystal Palace. Located well within the orbit of Detroit, the site was the fifty-eight acres occupied by the Highland Park Resort Hotel and racetrack. Since this area had been relatively slow in developing, it was possible to buy the land for $62,000, which was considered a "good" price. Moreover, since Henry Ford had been born here in Greenfield Township, and had worked in this area when he was a young boy, he was already familiar with the site, and undoubtedly knew that the tract of land fell where three railroads, the Michigan Central, the Grand Trunk, and the Detroit Terminal Railroad converged. Thus, it was in Highland Park on a plot of land covering about sixty acres that the Ford Motor Company institutionalized the production and assembly methods that would revolutionize automotive production.[41]

While Henry Ford and his associates were rightfully proud of their accomplishments at the Piquette Street plant, and considered that facility to be as good as, perhaps a little better than, any automobile factory in the world,[42] the Highland Park plant would be an even greater source of pride and satisfaction.[43] Ford "had visions of a factory layout all under one roof, eliminating the cartage of various components and bodies from their separate manufacturing sites to an assembly building. The manufacturing and assembly operations would be together in one huge building."[44] Albert Kahn was the architect who best understood and favored Ford's concept. So it was Kahn and his associate, Ernest Wilby (in close consultation with William B. Mayo and Edward Gray), who designed Ford's Highland Park plant, which quickly became known as the Crystal Palace.

The Crystal Palace was uniquely situated in both the spatial and temporal evolution of industrial technology; it was the largest automotive plant in its day—the main plant of Ford Motor Company for nearly twenty years and the entire life of the Model T. It "represented [the] full realization of the American system of production and the maturation of the modern industrial age," and "it transcended craft techniques in the metal and the carriage and wagon trades and moved toward the sophisticated, capital-intensive technologies of the auto-industrial age,"[45] and it "became the Mecca of industrialists from around the world."[46]

The extensive use of reinforced concrete, steel, and glass (with a minimum of brick) in industrial structures that were well lighted and well ventilated was first demonstrated by Albert Kahn in a group of Detroit factory buildings for the Packard Motor Car Company beginning in 1905. But the functional design of the Crystal Palace was advanced beyond anything previously known in the industry. In 1913 the chairman of the board of Dodge Brothers, Frederick J. Haynes, expressed the generally held view that the Ford Motor Company possessed the best factory arrangement for car production known in the United States. Similarly, F.L. Faurote, a noted author of books and articles on automobile manufacturing, declared that this facility was one of the most efficient plants he had seen anywhere; and having visited all of the principal manufacturers, Ford's construction engineer "was satisfied that the works were unequaled."[47] With the exception of a few ornamental bricks, the Crystal Palace was built of steel, concrete, and glass. On bright days the more than 50,000 square feet of glass allowed the structure to be flooded with sunlight. With its four stories, its length of 865 feet, about the length of two and two-thirds football fields, and breadth of 75 feet, the Crystal Palace was the largest building under one roof in Michigan.[48]

According to descriptions recorded around 1910, the Crystal Palace was unique, and quite different from previous factory construction. There was a craneway between each pair of buildings, and the roof of the craneway was glass so that the entire length of the building was showered with natural light. The heating and air-conditioning plant was on the roof, and the roof was also designed to ventilate the buildings. The waste air, on its way out, heated the craneway without added expense. The layout of the building facilitated the unloading and loading of freight cars. An especially imaginative innovation enabled raw materials to be hoisted as near the roof as possible, letting the work down in the process of manufacture. Thousands of holes were cut through the floors so that parts that started in rough form on the top floor gravitated down through chutes, conveyors, or tubes, and finally became a finished article on the ground floor.[49] Clearly, the innovations that would catapult the Ford Motor Company into its position as the leader among automotive manufacturers were to be found in both the design of the Crystal Palace, and in new uses of machine-tool technology.

During the next few years, Kahn designed a series of Ford plants across the United States and, later, the majority of the buildings of the Rouge complex, the largest in the world. Kahn also built the Dodge plant, and the Cadillac plant. All told, Kahn and his associates are estimated to have designed as many as a thousand buildings for Ford and nearly 20% of the major industrial buildings in the United States.[50] Undoubtedly the leading figure in his profession during the early 1900s, and thanks largely to his designs for the Ford Motor Company, Kahn is regarded by many as the greatest industrial architect who ever lived.

In a characteristically self-confident and poignant manner, the *Ford Times* noted that the move from the Piquette and Beaubien facility to the Crystal Palace was accomplished "without a brass band, a ball, a clambake, or even a speech from the mayor."[51] The move was quick and remarkably efficient: on December 31, 1909, the Ford Motor Company was shipping all of its cars from the Piquette plant, but on January 1, 1910, most of the cars were being shipped from the Crystal Palace. Extensive planning had assured that the department-by-department transfer would go smoothly. Although only about one-quarter of the Crystal Palace had been completed at the time of the transfer, production continued without interruption. The first part of the Crystal Palace to be finished housed the machine shop for making engines, transmissions, axles, and radiators, and the painting rooms, and the shipping rooms.

Automotive production in 1910 remained a relatively complicated, inefficient process consisting of four main operations: the foundry production of castings; machine-shop operations; the assembly of individual parts and components; and finally, the assembly of parts and components onto the chassis. Within the space of a few years, the Ford Motor Company rationalized these processes to achieve unprecedented efficiency in production; and thereby establish the Model T and the Crystal Palace as world leaders in automotive engineering and production.

Changes in Ford's manufacturing processes were aimed at developing and perfecting mass production. According to Henry Ford himself, "Mass production is focusing upon a manufacturing operation . . . of seven different principles: power, accuracy, economy, continuity, system, speed, and repetition."[52] The foundation upon which the seven principles were to be laid was standardization in product design, in this instance, meaning the standardization of the design of the Model T. Between 1908 and 1914 the Ford Motor Company implemented and perfected three types of innovations that led the way in revolutionizing industrial production in general, and automotive production in particular.

The first of the three innovations involved an increasingly specialized use of machinery in the production process and was consistent with manufacturing trends of the period. The second tier of innovations was based on the standardization of parts and components of the Model T, and included the more efficient organization, synchronization, and mechanization of the production and assembly processes. The third level of innovation, which will be discussed in more detail in the following chapter, was aimed at creating a new type of worker at every level of the production process, from the most skilled machine operator, down to the floor sweepers. Ford's Sociology Department, and the Ford Security Department, and the Americanization program were the agents that would invent and shape this new type of worker. The guaranteed minimum wage, popularly known as the five-dollar day, would be the incentive that would (according to the plan) persuade the worker to embrace his new identity as The Ford Man.

Building the Model T

Practically speaking, the process that ended with one thousand Model Ts arriving at the shipping departments of Ford plants, began with the men recognized as the "aristocracy" of the Ford Motor Company. Among these white-collar employees were 250 tool makers who, the management asserted, "are as good as can be found in the world." This corps of elites also included the 20 men working in the experimental room, the draftsmen, and "a large force of metal pattern makers in the foundry pattern room, all of whom must be first-class mechanics."[53] This white-collar aristocracy was the envy of many Ford workers, for it was known that many of those who had risen to the highest echelon of the Ford company had started with Ford as either tool makers, experimental hands, or draftsmen. For example, when "Henry Ford began at 81 Park Place in 1901, he worked as a machinist on the first Ford with his own hands and had with him one young machinist, one draughtsman, and one boy"; in 1914 the draughtsman had become the factory superintendent, the young machinist had become the chief inspector, and the former boy had become metallurgist-in-chief of the Highland Park plant.[54]

Each day, approximately 75 boxcars of parts and materials arrived by rail at the receiving department of the Highland Park plant; in a manner of speaking, it was with the arrival of these materials from outside suppliers that production actually began. The parts that arrived by rail included the wheels, tires, coil-box units, carburetors (Holley & Kingston), lamps, 90% of the car painting, all drop forging, all roller and ball bearings, grease cups, spark plugs, electric conductors, gaskets, hose connections and hose clips, the horn, fan belt, muffler pipe, and a considerable part of the bolts and nuts. In addition to the items noted above, the Model T bodies produced by the labor of several thousand men working in five separate locations were also shipped to the Crystal Palace.[55]

The materials coming to the Highland Park plant arrived by rail at the northeast side of the main plant, and after their inspection the receiving department, located near the northeast corner of the main building on John R. Street, forwarded them to the appropriate departments throughout the plant. Initially, these incoming materials were under the control of the stock superintendent who had direct supervisory authority over one assistant, six office clerks, and an army of departmental stock-keepers ("department receiving"), checkers, counters, stock handlers, truckers, and weighmasters—totaling about 1,285 men outside the office. In addition to his army of blue-collar workers, the stock superintendent had control of all traveling cranes and the electric monorail.

Beginning with the incoming-material inspectors, and continuing throughout the production process, inspectors represented the second tier of white-collar employees directly involved in the manufacture of the Model T. The chief inspector, who began as a machinist with the first Ford cars built in the shop at 81 Park Place during 1901 and 1902, had three assistant inspectors, two on the day shifts and one on the night shift, directly responsible to him. Among the 600 inspectors involved in the production of the Model T in 1914, there were 120 "incoming-material inspectors" who, on the basis of the Ford Motor Company's specifications and drawings, evaluated all material received from outside suppliers. In addition to the incoming-material inspectors, and the inspectors assigned to each of the departments, there were "operations inspectors" (perhaps the most feared of all) who routinely and at random inspected the work throughout the production process. In the foundry, there were 50 inspectors who inspected "every piece of casting made by the foundry, first in the rough, then as to tumbling, snagging, and visible defects and see that all work sent from the foundry to the machine shop is to all appearance satisfactory." Each of the machine-shops had one or more "machine-inspectors" (of which there are about 120 on the day shifts and 100 on the night shift) who moved from one machine to another inspecting work in progress. Machine-inspectors had a wide range of discretionary power. They could either advise the departmental foreman of a problem, order a change of tools or call a tool-setter to remedy the problem, or they could correct faulty tool-settings themselves. Most of the 100 night-shift inspectors were machine inspectors who operated in the same manner as those on the two day-shifts, but the night-shift also included six to eight "rejected components" inspectors and about 20 "scrap" or "wasters" inspectors whose sole purpose was to salvage parts when possible and to determine the source of faults in materials rejected by others. The "floor-" or "final-inspectors" graded, and usually tagged, finished parts.[56] Thus, beginning with the arrival of materials from outside suppliers, and continuing through the machine-shops and assembly processes, a corps of more than 600 inspectors worked to maintain a constant vigil over every aspect of the production in the Crystal Palace.

Always under the scrutiny of inspectors, Model T production may be seen as an ongoing process divided into three main phases that overlapped in both time and space. The first phase was the foundry where essentially raw materials were molded and prepared for further processing. The second and third phases consisted of a variety of machining and assembly operations as the components moved toward the shipping department. Machine-shop and assembly operations on crankshafts, cylinder blocks, pistons, front axles, and the chassis assembly were typical of related operations throughout the manufacturing process and are the basis for the following sketch of what the workmen made and how the work was done.

Foundry

The core-sand gallery, the mold carriers, and the endless chain core-ovens were what distinguished the foundry in the Crystal Palace from other foundries; but like most foundries that were part of a complex manufacturing process, the Ford foundry took in essentially unprocessed materials and began their preparation for subsequent distribution and refinement in other areas of the plant. Operation of the foundry was under the control of one supervisor, who had under his control a cadre of foremen, job-foremen, assistant foremen and straw bosses who supervised all aspects of foundry production.

The foundry was divided into five units. Each unit had its own overhead chute and two circuits of mechanically driven mold-carriers with a double line of molding machines fitted between them. Each unit had "molders; mold-handlers, who took molds from the machines and deposited them on the pendulum shelves of the carriers, or closed them on drags previously placed on the shelves; weight layers, who laid weights on the copes of the closed molds; pourers, who carried skimmers and skimmed their own hand-ladles; and shake-out men, who shook out the molds at the grating and piled the runners together."[57]

Except for the commutator-case, all Ford gray-iron, brass, and aluminum castings were made in the Highland Park foundry. Specifically, the five units made the following parts: unit 1 made exhaust end covers, exhaust pipes, reverse drums, intake pipes, valve heads and cam shaft bearings; unit 2 made brake shoes, reverse drums, slow speed, and brake drums; unit 3 made pistons, and piston pots; unit 4 made cylinder heads, water inlet connections, and exhaust pipes; unit 5, employing 65 men without machine moldings, made magneto spools, reverse drums, slow speed and brake drums. The cylinders were forged in a somewhat different process.

In addition to the five units noted above, the foundry had a cylinder-floor crew, which worked without the benefit of the mechanically driven mold-carriers. The cylinder molders were organized into thirteen gangs, each consisting of one cope rammer and one cope rammer's helper; one drag rammer and one drag rammer's helper; a drag finisher who inspected and finished the drag half of the mold and set three cylinder cores; a cope finisher who inspected and finished the cope half of the mold and set the water-jacket core; a barrel-core setter who set the barrel cores in the molds, gave it a final inspection, sealed, and with the help of bankers, closed the mold; and two bankers, who helped to close the molds, make the runner basins, and "bank up" the molds.[69] Four gangs were served by craneways No. 1 and No. 2, and five gangs served by craneway No. 3. Each craneway employed one pouring gang, including one pourer who also operated the crane, one pourer's helper, and one man who skimmed and assisted as required; each of the three crane-ways was serviced by one shaker-out gang consisting of one fore-man and 25 men. All counted, there were 466 workmen on the cylinder floor.

In 1914 the foundry employed a total of 1,450 men, and was in operation for three eight-hour shifts. About 55 men in the "job-bing" department were highly skilled molders who were said to be the best that could be obtained. Other molders and core-setters in the foundry were classified as "skilled." Approximately 95% of those employed in the foundry were "simply specialized laborers, many of them foreigners who had never seen the inside of a foundry and could speak no English when they began."[59] Gener-ally speaking, these foreigners "were given one piece only to put up." They "learned the 'trade' in two days . . . and began to turn out a full day's work of good castings on the third day of employ-ment." Those who "cannot learn to put up a small, plain job in two days the Ford foundry bosses pass him up as hopeless."[60]

Machine Shops

Machine shops were at the heart of Model T production and processed a great variety of parts. Some parts arrived in the machine shops from outside suppliers, and others came from the heat-treating ovens or the foundry in the Highland Park plant. In every case, whatever the origin of the parts arriving in the machine shops or the particular operation to be completed, the machine shop superintendent and his one assistant were ulti-mately responsible for all phases of work done in the machine shops, "the two working together in such absolute harmony" that Horace L. Arnold "was informed that they were of equal rank, which appears to be the truth in practice, though not in accor-dance with the register of officials."[61] Immediately below the superintendents in authority (and status) were the 11 machine-shop foremen, each in charge of separate departments, 62 job fore-men, 84 assistant foremen, and 98 subforemen, or straw bosses. Thus, there was a total of about 255 white-collar employees, "men above the rank of ordinary workmen," distributed throughout the machine shops who had direct supervisory authority over an army of common blue-collar workmen whose hands were directly involved in building the Model T.

In the same sense that innovative uses of jigs and fixtures and the uses of ever more powerful special-purpose machines were important in transferring skill from worker to machines in the production of parts like the Model T cylinder block and pistons, the synchronization of production processes was an important element in the development of continuous or progressive production. "Progressive production and progressive assembly involved the arrangement of men and machines and the coordination and synchronization of productive operations"; and this was, as Stephen Meyer has noted, the next logical step from the division of labor and the use of advanced specialized machine tools.[62] Progressive production began about 1912-1913 in the machine shops that produced finished metal parts, and then was gradually adapted to the assembly operations during 1913-1914.[63]

The guiding practice behind many early advances in the Ford machine shops was to "select, design and construct machine tools and attachments to match the skill level of the labor force," and "the innovative uses of jigs and fixtures were among the initial efforts to optimize the production of unskilled labor." Jigs and fixtures were work-holding devices that adapted multi-purpose and special-purpose machines for the high volume production of identical parts. Technically speaking, a jig held work but was not fastened to the machine. A fixture, often referred to as "furniture" or "appliance" by engineers, also held work but was fastened to the table or bed of the machine.[64] Thus, it was initially through the extensive use of jigs and fixtures that the Ford Motor Company was able to accomplish the high volume production of identical parts. While thousands of innovative jigs and fixtures remained in use, special use machines, such as those used in the production of the Model T cylinder block, crank shaft, pistons, etc., became increasingly important.

As described by Arnold and Faurote, progressive production was the scheme of placing both machine and hand at work in a straight line sequence of operations, so that the component in progress traveled the shortest road from start to finish, with no avoidable handling whatever. In order to achieve the constant and continuous movement of raw materials, parts, and components, it was necessary for Ford engineers to develop many new devices. These included gravity work-slides and rollways that moved work by hand, endless chains and endless conveyor belts, and overhead cranes that moved parts from one work station to another. The applications of innovations such as these to the production and assembly of the magneto and chassis are excellent examples of both the pace and the significance of innovations which originated and were perfected in the Crystal Palace.

The pace of the revolution in the Crystal Palace accelerated on April 1, 1913, with the installation of the first sliding assembly line in the flywheel magneto department. The results were spectacular, and discussions about other possible applications immediately ensued. The revolution quickly spread throughout the Ford plants as workmen (white-collar and blue-collar) adapted the principle of placing the most suitable components on elevated ways or rails that carried the components past successive stationary sources of parts, and past successive groups of workmen who affixed the various parts to the moving component.[66] These principles were first extensively applied with the flywheel magneto.

The flywheel magneto provided the electrical charge to ignite the fuel in the Model T and was the first component to be assembled on the moving assembly line. The assembly of the magneto changed radically between May 1913 and March 1914. By May 1913, it was normal for one skilled worker to assemble from thirty-five to forty magnetos in a nine-hour day. According to Arnold, the assembly was done by experienced men, "but was not uniformly satisfactory as desired, and was costly . . . as all one-man assembly must of necessity be forever."[67] In May of 1913, Ford managers and engineers subdivided the task into twenty-nine separate operations and added a chain-driven conveyor to move the magneto from one worker to another. With continued experimentation and modification, productivity increased dramatically; by the end of March 1914, fourteen workers assembled 1,335 magnetos in an eight-hour day. Thus, "even though the working day was reduced by one hour, the assemblers more than doubled their average productivity and produced an average of ninety-five magnetos per person each day."[68] Similar strides toward increased efficiency and output were made in finishing the crank shaft.

Crankshaft: The crankshaft arrived in the crankshaft department after it had already received four heat-treatments. The mechanical operations began when one hammer and two tong-men "re-struck" the shaft, after which two men placed the shafts into a tumbling barrel, and then five men, using emery stands, snagged about 150 shafts per hour. In the next operation, one hammer-man and three gauge-men rough-straightened the shafts, which then went to the "machine-shop finish-straightening gang which consisted of three strikers who used eighteen-pound sledges to strike the shafts which were held on three anvils by gauge-men." The next step was mostly a machining operation in which the middle bearing was turned on Reed lathes; with one man on each of five lathes, twenty-five center-bearings were "rough turned" per hour. With each succeeding operation (about twenty-nine in all, including centering, drilling, grinding, finish-grinding, balancing, and the final operation, polishing) the crank-shaft moved ever closer to its final inspection in this department and the assembly line. Regarding the quality of workmanship in the crankshafts, Arnold and Faroute confidently stated that, "if the Ford crankshafts are not well finished the faults cannot be charged to any lack of painstaking on the part of the machine shop management."[69]

Cylinder Block: Similar savings were achieved in the assembly of the Model T engine. In the early days at Ford, the engine block was passed by hand from one work station to another in order to have various operations performed.[70] This process was apparently inefficient and "finally the motor-assembling foreman analyzed the time with a stop watch and found that four hours out of a nine-hour day were spent in walking—that is to say, in body movements of each assembler made by moving his feet."[71] The addition of some carefully placed new machines would help to eliminate much of the unnecessary "walking." The Foote-Burt Company made a number of special use machines for the Ford Motor Company. Among these were machines built especially for drilling the Model T cylinder block and for machining pistons. The Foote-Burt multiple drilling machine was arranged to simul-taneously drill all forty-five holes in the cylinder block. As described by Abell and Colvin, the process was quite simple: "The cylinder is jigged into position, the operator throws the starting lever, the machine is equipped with automatic stop and reverse, the operator takes the cylinder out and the work is done." In this manner, forty-five separate operations were accomplished with one special-purpose machine.[72]

From the first to the last operation, (the first was to put the cylinders on hot plates and plug holes with asbestos, and the last was painting the motor and removing it from the line) the motor assembly required eighty-four separate operations, employing the hands of one hundred men. The new system resulted in such a savings of labor so that on May 8, 1914, one motor was assembled in 226 minutes of one man's time as against nearly 594 minutes in November of 1913. The motor-block test completed the motor assembly. As of June, 1914, this test employed Westinghouse elec-tric motors that turned the engines at 750 rpm for three to five minutes. Manpower on this operation consisted of twenty-one men, including one head block tester, one assistant, and one tester for each of the nineteen Westinghouse electric motors. Following the test, the engine, along with its assembler's record, was sent to the assembly line.[73]

Pistons: Improvements in the production of Model T pistons also serve to demonstrate how special-use machines were used during the early phase of skilled worker displacement. Except for placing the casting on the inverted spindle and starting the machine, the machining of pistons had become entirely automated. According to Colvin's 1913 description, the top of the pistons were faced off at the same time that the outside diameter was being turned and three piston-ring grooving tools were automatically fed to the required depth. The feed was automatically tripped, and the cutters were automatically returned to their starting position. Therefore, all the machine operator had to do was to release the clamp holding the pistons in position, slip out the retaining pins, and put another piston on the spindle.[74]

In the piston and connecting-rod assembling department (following the foreman's stopwatch analysis) fourteen men were able to produce the same number of finished pistons as twenty-eight men had produced two months earlier. In addition to the increased level of production that resulted from innovations in the assembly process, the employment of an inspector who guaged and inspected each piston and rod assembly resulted in the virtual elimination of "spoiled" or "rejected" parts from the motor assembling line.[75]

Front Axle Components Finishing & Assembly

As of July 9, 1914, the front-axle components finishing department had approximately 375 blue-collar workers under the supervision of one foreman who was "of necessity, a competent mechanic and a competent administrator," two assistant foremen, and one straw boss for every 20 workmen (17-18 straw bosses). The department also had tool-setters who were "machinists of intelligence, experience, and all-round reliability,"[76] and three clerks. This cast of white-collar, and would-be white-collar, elites supervised the finishing processes on the front axle.

Before arriving in the finishing department, the axle had already been heat-treated, annealed, rough-straightened, and snagged and tumbled; while in the department, each of the (approximately) eighteen main parts of the axle, often using specialized machine-tools, went through from four to fourteen separate steps which included some combination of drilling, burring, turning, punching, threading, reaming, brazing, grinding, riveting, inspecting, etc. When finished, the axle was sent by monorail to the front-axle assembly department.

Improvements in the front-axle assembly department of the Crystal Palace were typical of the reductions in labor costs achieved by improvements in machine tools and the more efficient organization of work. More specifically, on January 1, 1913, it required an average of 150 minutes of one man's time to assemble one front axle, and on January 1, 1914, it required 66.5 minutes; but on July 13, 1914, about six weeks after the moving-assembly which had begun operation on June 1, 1914, front axles were assembled in 26.5 minutes.[77]

During the period 1913-1914, Clarence Avery was the principal agent in the coordination and synchronization of production in the various departments of the Crystal Palace. By the end of 1914 Avery and his staff had succeeded throughout the plant in replicating the pattern of increased efficiency seen in the magneto department. After about an eight-month period during which the production routines in each of the departments were analyzed, the necessary timing schedules were worked out, and one by one those operations were revamped so that continuously moving conveyors delivered assembled parts to the final assembly floor. The resulting efficiency in production was phenomenal; in some instances parts were put together six times faster.

Chassis Assembly

The ultimate challenge during the period 1913-1914 was the chassis assembly. It was the chassis line to which the thousands of parts and components flowed, and it was here that they would be assembled to the chassis, and here that the Model T would take its shape. According to the recollection of one worker, in 1903 the assembly of automobiles at the Ford Motor Company was entirely manual. The cars were assembled on the spot, to which the chassis, the motor and the body were brought. "As near as I can remember," said the worker, the body was brought on a hand truck, and was lifted up and placed onto the chassis, and after the car was assembled, "one fellow would take hold of the rear end and one of the front end, and they'd lift the whole thing up! . . . I would say there would be just one or two men for each assembly, as near as I can remember."[78] The chassis assembly procedures apparently did not change significantly in the decade between 1903 and 1913.

Prior to introduction of the moving assembly process (up to August 1913), the chassis was assembled at fifty locations and required the hands of six-hundred men (five-hundred assemblers and one-hundred component-carriers). At each of the fifty locations, the front and rear-axles were laid on the floor, and then the chassis frame with springs in place was assembled with the axles; next the wheels were placed on the axles and the remaining components, all brought by hand to each assembly location, were successively added until the chassis was ready for the test driver.[79] The practice "was to let the driver run the chassis up and down until he thought best to abandon it" to the motor and rear-axle inspectors, and to return to the end of the assembling lines for another chassis to drive out onto John R Street."[80]

The final step was to place bodies onto the chassis; the "bodies were allowed to slide down an incline from the second floor, and were then dragged along the pavement by one man and stood on end in a bunch south of the chute." After inspection, the vehicle chassis was again driven to the "bunch of bodies, where four men lifted a body onto the chassis, and the completed automobile was driven to the shipping-clerk's office, between the railway tracks, ready for shipment."[81]

H.L. Arnold's description of the Model T chassis assembly process in 1913 lends further support to the contention that little in this process had changed since 1903. According to Arnold, "First, the front and rear axles were laid on the floor, then the chassis frame with springs in place were assembled with the axles, next the wheels were placed on the axles, and the remaining components were successively added to complete the chassis."[82] With this method of assembly, 250 skilled assemblers with the assistance of non-skilled component carriers were able to assemble 6,182 chassis per month; at this rate, the assembly of one chassis required an average of 12.5 workman hours.

In August of 1913, Ford managers and engineers had begun the experimentation that would synchronize chassis assembly with the already improved production of thousands of parts and components that were combined to make the Model T. In September of that year, engineers had experimented with a rope and windlass, which was used to pull the Model T chassis along a row of parts and components. As the chassis moved along the rows, six skilled assemblers, accompanied by their helpers, walked alongside the moving chassis and attached the various parts. This rope-and-windlass technique lessened chassis assembly time 50%, to about 5.8 hours per chassis. Additional improvements followed in October.

In October, Ford engineers mechanically pulled the chassis along a line of 140 stationary assemblers who stood near supplies of parts that they attached to the passing chassis; this innovation further reduced chassis assembly time to slightly less than three hours per worker. Before the end of 1913, changes in the length of the assembly line and the number of assembler-stations resulted in greater efficiency. The "endless chain-driven" conveyor that was developed in January, and the April 1914 modifications that introduced the "man-high line" (i.e., work stations raised or lowered so that they were about waist high) to eliminate more of the unnecessary and non-productive movements of workers, marked the last in the series of experiments and innovations that combined to reduce chassis assembly time from 12.5 hours to 1.55 hours

The net result was a vastly improved assembly system, "believed to show the very first example of minutely divided assembling operations on so large a unit as an automobile."[93] Powered by chain-driven conveyors, the chassis assembly began at the south end of the assembly department and moved northward, passing under the overhead gasoline-tank platform, the motor-carrying chain-hoist tracks, the dash assembly platform, and the radiator platform.

The moving-assembly speed was varied to suit exactly each separate assembling job as the chassis, growing component by component, moved past each assembler or gang of assemblers; the dash-assembly moved at 72 inches per minute, the front axle at 189, the body-and-top assembly at 144, and the chassis at 72. Work was divided so that assemblers had 7 minutes 36 seconds to complete an operation, and the department completed an average of six chassis in eight hours (three hundred on each line). As described by Arnold and Faurote, the moving-assembly process involved forty-five separate operations, including the following steps: two men completed fixing combined front fender-irons and lamp brackets; two men placed motor and connected the universal joint of the propeller shaft to the change-gear shaft; one man placed spark plugs; two men placed the dash assembly; one man placed and fixed the commutator; one man pinned steering-gear bracket nut, and adjusted spark time; two men put on wheels and placed wheel nuts; one man tightened radiator water connection; and one man drove the car on to John R Street. As soon as a chassis was driven onto the John R track the clutch was adjusted so that, with the motor running, the chassis would "creep" southward toward the body chute. After the clutch was adjusted, the water connection to the radiator was checked for leaks and tightened if necessary; after inspection, the top nut of the steering shaft was put on, followed by a careful adjustment of the carburetor; the motor inspector then "put the motor through its paces." Finally, the rear-axle inspection took place under the body chute, and if everything was in order, the chassis was sent to the south end of the chute where a body was placed on it; the completed car was then ready to be driven out to the shipping platform.[94]

Although each of the machine shops and component-assembly departments performed one or more unique operations, the patterns and routines of work (both the actual work requiring the hands of blue-collar workers, and the "mental" work of white-collar supervisors and managers) had much in common. Broadly speaking, Arnold and Faurote's comments regarding the commutator department appear appropriate to the production of other parts as well: "Constant supervision of workmen, constant work inspection, and constant watching of tool-cuts by the tool-setters, give skilled overlooking to the work of every man on the commutator job." Many of the machine hands in the commutator department, more than in some other areas of the factory, "though not regular machinists, are highly skilled and grind and set their own tools." Moreover, "every workman is perfectly aware that he is under constant observation, and that he will be admonished if he falls below the fast pace of the department."[95] The head of the commutator department stated, "I depend largely on my tool-setters for my production. The tool-setters know exactly what I want, and as long as the tool-setters have plenty of newly sharpened tools on hand, all ready to go into machines as soon as tools in use show loss of smooth-cutting edge, I have no trouble in keeping my production up to the 1750 per 8 hours mark. But if there is even a small delay in replacing a cutting tool which does not work exactly right, trouble begins."[96]

According to Arnold and Faurote, who were given privileged access to the factory in 1914, with the exception of "the matter of ventilation," all working conditions in the foundry are the very best. "[C]old pure water is everywhere at hand, goggles and leather leggings are supplied by the company to those liable to accident from molten metal, and no workman is worked beyond a reasonable exertion of muscular powers."[97] The introduction of automatic mold-carriers contributed to the clean floor in unit 4, and had contributed to everything preceding in good "factory form"; but the cylinder department, to which the automatic mold-carriers had not yet been extended, "shows the unusual conditions, everybody working at disadvantage in an atmosphere of smoke and steam."[98] More generally, reported Arnold and Faurote, "the ventilation is now far from what it should be; the air during work hours cannot be endured by any workman save those possessing respiratory organs of the most robust description, and many visitors are unable to walk through the Ford gray-iron foundry in working hours because they cannot breathe the air."[99]

On the basis of their observations, Arnold and Faurote noted that despite the foremen and sub-foremen who "find it hard to accept instruction" and the workmen who are always suspicious of the "speed-up," the high wage does away with any resistance and the "workmen are absolutely docile."[100] Evidence (perhaps) of how well the unskilled foundry workers had adapted to the Ford system may be seen in the statistic that of the 1,450 workers on the foundry pay-roll, about 1,200 were receiving $5.00 or more for eight hours work. Whatever the state of ventilation or the degree of dissatisfaction, management "got the work out" and the mono-rail tracks smoothly entered the foundry at the southeast corner and took the foundry product to the machine-shops.

3

Technological Innovation
and the Demographic Transformation
of Highland Park

The growth and expansion of the Ford Motor Company were directly associated with the introduction of the moving assembly line and brought about the demographic transformation of the Detroit region. This transformation can be seen by an analysis of the composition of the workforce in Ford's Crystal Palace, and in Highland Park and its neighboring communities. The analysis is based primarily on the 1910, 1920, and 1930 United States Census reports, and a special census of the population of Highland Park conducted by the United States Census Bureau during November 1915.[1]

Before examining the details of the demographic transformation of Highland Park, it should be noted that the demographic changes in the Detroit region were part of a larger trend. More precisely, the shift in location and composition of the United States population may be described as part of a worldwide phenomenon often described as "the demographic transition." The years between 1890 and 1920 were the approximate period in which the United States and Europe reached the "modern state," characterized by a slow-growing population.[2] For the United States, the transition has meant that during each decade since 1860 the population has become more native-born (except 1860-1870), less black, and more female. And, in every decade since 1860 (except 1940-1970) the population has also contained a growing proportion of adults and a smaller proportion of persons under the age of twenty. Value added in manufacture per capita has also risen with each decade since 1860.[3] Within this larger context the demographic transformation of Highland Park and its vicinity may be understood.

Table 3.1
Detroit Region (BEA # 71) Population Characteristics
Including: Percent Foreign Born, Percent Black,
Ratio of Males to Females, Percent Adult Population,
Value Added Per Capita in Manufacture 1860-1960

Year	%Foreign Born	%Black	Males/ Females	%Adults	$Mfg/ Per Capita	Population
1860	26.7	1.1	106.8	49.4	18	272,992
1870	28.7	1.3	105.3	50.4	45	375,617
1880	28.3	1.2	104.3	52.8	39	472,662
1890	29.5	1.0	101.6	55.5	67	577,529
1900	25.6	1.0	100.4	58.0	96	687,484
1910						
1920	25.1	3.0	116.6	62.7	660	1,649,460
1930	21.0	5.6	109.6	61.6	537	2,636,967
1940	16.7	6.3	104.7	65.1	392	2,886,605
1950						
1960	8.8	13.3	97.9	59.2	1137	4,582,233

Source: Sam Bass Warner and Sylvia Fleisch, *Measurements for Social History*, Sage (1977) excerpts from "Appendix B." Warner and Fleisch noted that the exact data employed in their book are on computer tape as "Socieconomic Indicators for Functional Urban Regions in the United States 1820-1970" (ICPSR #7506), and are available to members of the Inter-University Consortium.

Warner and Fleisch's analysis of the demographic transition of the United States includes the generalization that "During the nineteenth century maleness was not strongly associated with manufacturing in areas one way or the other, but since 1920 the two have increasingly diverged."[4] Table 3.1 suggests that this generalization either does not apply to the Detroit region, or perhaps that the statistics need to be refined. More precisely, the period of increase in "manufacturing" ($Mfg/Per Capita in Table 3.1) was also a time during which the male to female ratio showed the greatest difference. This is clearly contrary to the national trend and Warner and Fleisch's expectations. For the purposes of this study, what is important is that the apparent inconsistencies of their generalizations with the historic pattern of manufacturing

Model T Assembly: Men installing pistons   (From the Collections of Henry Ford Museum & Greenfield Village)

and the composition of the population of the Detroit region support the assertion that an understanding of the economic history of the region can come only from a study of the cities and towns that make up the region—cities such as Highland Park and Hamtramck, both located in close proximity to the Crystal Palace Ford plant.

Warner and Fleisch further generalize that "During the twentieth century concentrations of women and factories are found more and more together. [Moreover] one might note that femaleness and factories and big cities are three characteristics postulated as the companions of the modern stage of demographic transition."[5] Here again, Warner and Fleisch's observation seems contrary to that realized in the Detroit region. For example, femaleness in the Motor City does not become dominant until the era of deindustrialization is well under way.[6] In each instance, Warner and Fleisch's generalizations confirm the need to further disaggregate the social statistics of the region, thus enabling a closer focus on communities like Highland Park, and the more thorough analysis of various groups inhabiting such communities. Therefore, with the reminder that the transformation occurred within a larger national and regional context, this study now turns to a consideration of the expansion of the Ford Motor Company and the resulting demographic transformation of Highland Park.

With the establishment of the Olds Motor Company in 1899, followed by Cadillac in 1902, Ford, Packard, and Hupp in 1903, and Hudson in 1904, the foundation for Detroit's automotive future was in place. Beginning with Ford's high-volume, low cost production of the Model T, the sustained growth of Detroit and the automotive industry was assured. Detroit became "a place where—more than anyplace in the United States—the industrial society was changing the way people lived."[7]

Among the many fundamental changes coming in the wake of innovations leading to automated production and assembly technology, the demographic transformation of Detroit and its environs is one of the most easily identified. In 1900 Detroit was a city of 285,284 people, most of whom lived in ethnic neighborhoods near the Detroit River. Census reports show that by 1910 the population had grown to approximately 993,000, and by 1930 to 1,720,000. While the population of Detroit practically doubled during each of the three decades after 1900, the city also increased its territorial base. The annexation of outlying lands increased the size of the city from 28.35 square miles in 1900 to more than 40 square miles in 1910, and to more than 80 square miles in 1920. Both the increase in population and the expansion of the city boundaries were pushed by the automotive industry.[8]

A major component in the demographic transformation of the Detroit region was the appearance of black immigrants who presented a somewhat different challenge than that posed by the ethnics. With the exception of the automobile industry there was, perhaps, no element that played a greater role in giving Detroit its ultimate identity than the arrival of the black population.

Black immigrants in significant numbers first appeared in Michigan about 1840. At this time there were 707 Negroes in Michigan and 193 in Detroit, and by 1850 the number had increased to 2,283 and 587, respectively. Among these migrants was a small colony of ex-slaves who settled in Cass County, but the largest settlement of blacks, nearly one-quarter of Michigan's black population, lived in Detroit in 1850. Most of these early settlers were descended from free Negro migrants from urban centers in the state of Virginia; they came from Richmond, Fredericksburg, and Petersburg.[9] When contrasted with the waves of blacks who would arrive later, these early migrants were but a mere splash in an ocean of black souls who came in search of better lives.

These immigrants were pushed from the socially and economically inhospitable conditions in their home states, principally Alabama, Georgia, Florida and Tennessee;[10] in some cases floods and boll-weevil pests had made it virtually impossible for those who emigrated to make a living.[11] Their movement was vigorously stimulated by labor agents who were seeking to supply the labor needs of a rapidly growing city; the agents enticed the willing migrants with offers of free transportation, promises of higher wages, improved working conditions, and greater social freedom.[12]

The vast majority of black people who came to the Detroit area came in one of two waves. The first wave was part of the "great migration," which brought blacks during 1916-1917 to alleviate a labor shortage that resulted from the fact that World War I had disrupted the flow of immigrants who normally might have been expected to meet the labor needs,[13] and the fact that certain other members of the workforce had been drafted or had volunteered to do military service. The second wave in 1924-1925 brought a few like Ossian Sweet, and many thousands of others, especially single black men in their prime, to fill a vacuum in the labor force created by legislation restricting immigration into the United States.[14]

The immigration of blacks to the Detroit area was part of a larger, more complex movement that Donald has described as a social phenomenon representing the maladjustment of 500,000 Negroes.[15] Generally speaking, the northern and western parts of the United States saw an increase in the black population from 1,078,336 in 1910 to 1,550,754 in 1920, an increase of 472,418 or approximately 44%. Within the context of this movement, Michigan experienced an increase in the Negro population of 251%, that is from 17,115 in 1910 to 60,082 by 1920. Of this number, 35,097 migrated to Detroit and most others settled in southeastern communities.[16] More than any other city in Michigan, Detroit attracted the migrants; specifically, the city's increase in the black population was an astounding 623.4 percent, that is from 5,751 in 1910 to 41,532 in 1920.[17] What is important is that during this period the percentage increase of Detroit's black population was the highest in the nation, followed by Cleveland, Ohio, with an estimated increase of 307%, while no other urban community in the United States of more than 25,000 blacks in 1920 had increased more than 150%.[18]

This massive movement of manpower from the South to Detroit was often viewed with alarm.[19] The *Detroit News* sensationalized the "great migration" in articles and editorials in which the message was clear: "Negroes Open Drive On City. Advance Contingents of 50,000 Southerners Expected by Summer, Arrive Daily."[20] In another report the *News* declared in an editorial that the natural home of the Negro was in the South and that the South should revise its racial policies and call "him" back.[21] Despite the admonition of the *News*, for the time being, blacks did not in significant numbers return to the South; quite the contrary, the flood of migrants continued. Forrester B. Washington, the first head of the Detroit branch of the Urban League, reported that in May, June, and July of 1914, "1,000 Negroes a month were arriving in the city"; by 1920 it was estimated that over 1,000 blacks were arriving each week.[22] During the month of May in 1920, Washington sent an Urban League worker to meet the three trains that daily brought the majority of the migrants, and the count at the train station revealed the totals in table 3.2.

Noting that by the fall of 1916 a massive wave of black immigrants had begun to arrive in Detroit, Richard W. Thomas estimated that a total of 25,000 arrived in 1916-1917.[23] Remarkably,

Model T Assembly: Women assembling magnetos   (From the Collections of Henry Ford Museum & Greenfield Village)

then, the vast majority of the more than 40,000 blacks counted in 1920 had come to Detroit in one year. The second wave coming in 1924-1925 brought in over 40,000 additional blacks; thus by 1926, 85% of the black population had come to Detroit during the decade between 1916 and 1926. Both waves of immigration were closely associated with the increase in the value of Detroit's manufacturing products, resulting from the rapid industrial expansion of 1914.

Table 3.2
Urban League's Count of Black Immigrants to Detroit: May 1920

Monday May 3	216
Tuesday May 4	245
Wednesday May 5	215
Thursday May 6	274
Friday May 7	272
Saturday May 8	217
Sunday May 9	371
Total	1,810

Source: Forrester B. Washington, "The Negro in Detroit: A Survey of the Conditions of a Negro Group in a Northern Industrial Center During the War Prosperity Period," Detroit: Research Bureau, Associated Charities of Detroit, 1920.

In order to insure a sufficient supply of labor to feed the growing needs of the automotive industry, corporate and public officials were aggressive in their efforts to attract workers to the Detroit area. As early as August 1907, the Detroit Board of Commerce asked immigration officials at New York's Ellis Island to steer foreign workers to the city, and the Employer's Association of Detroit advertised in nearly 200 newspapers in order to entice workers to come to Detroit.[24] It appears that the Employer's Association served as something of a labor trust for area manufacturers. It may be argued, then, that the comparatively rapid increase in the size and the composition of Detroit's population was a direct reflection of response to the labor needs of the automotive industry. As Sydney Glazer states, "In 1908 the automotive industry in the city gave employment to 7,200 workers. In 1909 some

17,000 were employed. . . . By 1915 the figure increased to 81,000. In 1916, even prior to America's entrance into World War I, the industry employed 120,000 persons,"[25] and by 1920 that figure had risen to 135,000. If nothing else, these statistics (see Tables 3.3 and 3.4) should leave the impression of the rapidity with which the automotive industry and the population of the Detroit region grew.

Table 3.3
Rough Approximations of Major Racial and Ethnic Groups
in Detroit 1910 and 1930

1910		1930	
Group	Percent	Group	Percent
Polish	?	Polish	13
German	29	Canadian	11
Canadian	16	German	8
Russian	6	black	7
Austrian	5	Italian	4
Irish	4	English	4
English	4	Russian	3
Italian	2	Irish	2
Hungarian	2	Hungarian	1
black	1	Yugoslavian	1
Scottish	1	Czechoslovakian	1
Belgian	1	Austrian	1
		Greek	.5
		Finnish	.5
		Mexican	.5
		Syrian/Lebanese	.5
Foreign Born or Children of Foreign Born			
345,000	74	1,108,000	100%
Total Population			
466,000	100%	1,720,000	100%

Source: Steve Babson, *Working Detroit*, 1984: 27.

Table 3.4
Number of Foreign Born Whites by Country of Birth:
Highland Park 1920 and 1930

Country of Birth	1920	1930
Armenia	606	442
Austria	537	121
Belgium	8	25
Bulgaria	37	24
Canada (French)	119	333
Canada (Other)	3609	4043
Czechoslovakia	113	114
Denmark	97	61
England	1445	2660
Finland	102	174
France	87	90
Germany	558	521
Greece	253	181
Hungary	559	136
Ireland	417	436
Italy	970	979
Yugoslavia	282	339
Lithuania	40	35
Netherlands	45	40
Norway	79	82
Poland	30	219
Rumania	473	356
Russia	580	312
Scotland	411	1250
Sweden	180	199
Switzerland	33	47
Syria/Palestine	500	360
Wales	50	64
Mexico	7	0
Spain	0	22
Turkey	0	514
All Others	234	183
Totals	12,661	14,362

Source: United States Department of Commerce. Bureau of Census, *Abstract of the Fourteenth and Fifteenth Census of the United States*, 1920 and 1930.

Model T Assembly: Men installing tires   (From the Collections of Henry Ford Museum & Greenfield Village)

While all of the major immigrant groups were present among the industry's new workers, not all groups were equally represented. Not all of the automotive manufacturers got their "fair share" of immigrant workers, and not all neighborhoods received the new arrivals in equal proportions. Therefore, in order to comprehend how the automotive industry is related to demographic change in the Detroit region, it is necessary to disaggregate further the statistics shown in Table 3.1. As inferred from Warner and Fleisch, the basic question is this: Where did the Crystal Palace and Highland Park and neighboring communities fit into the settlement patterns of Detroit; and more pointedly, "What is the changing distribution of population and economic activities within a changing area?"[26] In other words, while the emphasis here is on Highland Park, it should be understood that the changes discussed here are part of a larger, more complex regional transformation. On this basis then, giving special attention to changes in total population, color, and ethnic origin, and male/female ratio and age composition, this study now turns to an analysis of the 1900-1930 census reports for Highland Park.

Table 3.2 shows that the percentage of foreign-born whites in the population of the Detroit region ranged from a high of 29.5% in 1890, and down to 25.6% in 1900 and 25.1% in 1920. The United States Census shows that the foreign-born white population in Highland Park was 27.2 in 1920, and 27.1 in 1930. Generally speaking, for the period under consideration, the proportion of foreign-born whites in Highland Park approximated that of the Detroit region. Furthermore, cursory inspection of Tables 3.1 and 3.3 reveals that Canada provided Highland Park with its largest contingent of immigrants in both the 1920 (28.5%) and 1930 (28.1%) censuses; and England provided the largest number of foreign-born whites in both 1920 and 1930 reports, at 9.0 and 18.4%, respectively. Italians ranked third (7.6%) in the 1920 census, and were the fourth most numerous (6.8%) in the 1930 census. Table 3.3 clearly shows that all of the major immigrant groups were represented in the Highland Park population, and that English-speaking countries (Canada and England in the period from 1910 and 1930, and Scotland in the decade of 1920-1930) were most prominent as points of origin, and that Italy sent a significant immigrant population for the entire period. It is worth noting that English-speaking countries and Italy provided a greater proportion of immigrants to Highland Park than to the region as a whole (compare data in Tables 3.3 and 3.4). Although immigrants often lived in ethnic neighborhoods that had been well established by 1900, there was a considerable variety in settlement patterns.

Table 3.5
Total Population of Highland Park for 1910, 1920 and 1930
By Sex, Race and Ratio of Males to Females over 21 Years of Age

	Total Population	#Males	#Females	Males 21+	Females 100	21+/ Females
1930	52,595	27,367	25,592			
1920	46,499	25,565	20,483	17,971	13,494	133.7
1915	27,170	14,721	12,499	10,060	8,052	124.9
1910	4,120	2,162	1,958	1,233	1,287	95.8
Native White						
1930	51,680					
1920	33,394	17,707	15,687	11,191	9,387	119.2
1915	27,100	14,687	14,413	10,031	8,024	125.0
1910	4,105	2,151	1,954	1,226	1,284	95.0
Black						
1930	1,171	585	586			
1920	358	193	165	133	11	
1915	57	24	33	19	26	
1910	15	11	4	7	3	

Source: United States Department of Commerce, Bureau of the Census. Thirteenth, Fourteenth and Fifteenth Census Reports: "Michigan Census," and the "Special Census of the Population of Highland Park, Michigan, November 15, 1915." The male/100 females ratios are based on these reports and computed by the author.

Highland Park and the Crystal Palace are excellent, perhaps the best, examples of how during the early decades of the twentieth century demographic change in the region is directly related to the rise of the automotive empire. "At the time of Ford's arrival in Highland Park its population was approximately 425 persons, but within a year it soared to 4,120. [F]ollowing Ford's announcement in January 1914 of the five-dollar minimum daily wage, the

Map 3.1

The City of Highland Park, Wayne County, Michigan
Showing Boundaries of Enumeration Districts at the Special Census
November 15, 1915
Boundaries are indicated by a heavy black line: ———

number of residents increased to 46,499 in 1920."[27] This "wonderful" increase in population made Highland Park one of the biggest population gainers in the whole country.[28] The subsequent decline in Highland Park's population was equally precipitous and was directly associated with the first restructuring and relocation of the Ford Motor Company. The rate of increase slowed in the decade of the 1920s, reached a peak of 52,959 by the 1930 census, and began a decline that reduced the population to 50,810 in 1940. By 1980 the population of Highland Park had dropped to 27,909, a level that approximated the 1915 level of 27,170.[29]

The rate of change in Highland Park's population is indeed remarkable. According to a tally taken by village officials in 1914, there were 22,000 residents in Highland Park. At the request of the village council, the request having been made through the village attorney to President Woodrow Wilson, the United States Bureau of the Census conducted a special census of the village of Highland Park. The special census began on November 15, 1915, and was completed in six days; this count revealed that the population of the village was 27,170. During the period between the 1914 tally and the special census of 1915, Highland Park gained 5,170 residents, an increase of 23.5%. But during the five years and seven months between the decennial census of 1910 and the special census of November 1915, Highland Park gained 23,050 residents—an increase of approximately 559.5%.

Given that both Highland Park and Hamtramck owed their growth almost exclusively to the automotive industry, and given that these two communities shared a boundary, the contrasts in their settlement patterns are especially interesting. Both Highland Park and Hamtramck are independent cities with the city limits of Detroit. With the Dodge Brothers plant as the driving force, Hamtramck grew from a village of a few hundred people in 1900, to a city of 48,615 in 1920, and to 56,268 in 1930.[30] The population increases in Hamtramck and Highland Park were very similar in number, but the settlement patterns were completely different. Steve Babson notes, for example, that although English-speaking immigrants were dispersed throughout the area, there was a greater than usual concentration in Highland Park. Adding to the existing English-speaking community, "The new Ford plant in Highland Park attracted nearby colonies of Finns, Yugoslavs, Rumanians, and Lithuanians, while the Dodge Brothers' sprawling plant in Hamtramck drew Polish immigrants north from Poletown."[31]

In an analysis of occupational stratification and residential segregation in Detroit and its surrounding communities, Olivier Zunz noted the contrasts between Highland Park and Hamtramck: Hamtramck was a working-class community dominated by one ethnic group. In Hamtramck, 65.8% of the heads of household were Polish, and another 4% native-born Americans of Polish parents; 85% were factory workers, 43% skilled or semiskilled and 42% unskilled, and a few held white-collar positions, mostly as shopkeepers. In short, Hamtramck was an extension of Detroit's Polish community.

Highland Park was completely different. Even though the Ford Motor Company employed many immigrants and more blacks than any of the other auto companies, Highland Park was inhabited primarily by native white American and other Anglo-Saxon workers. In a sample of 202 heads of households, only two were Polish, one Hungarian, and one black. Among the workers employed in manufacturing, 60% were classified as skilled. Of Highland Park households 42% were headed by native white Americans, or more generally, Anglo-Saxon white-collar workers. As Zunz notes, "Parts of Highland Park, then, were made up of residences of an ethnically homogeneous group of workers, different from that of neighboring Hamtramck, and another part of it was a middle-class neighborhood."[32]

Zunz's description of Hamtramck and Highland Park shows that while these two cities were similar in some important ways, there were significant differences. Especially interesting is the apparent fact that Hamtramck was an ethnically homogenous community in which residential segregation was based on class (i.e., occupational status). Highland Park, on the other hand, was ethnically more heterogeneous and consisted of two communities, one of which may be described as primarily WASP and white-collar. The other community may be described as ethnically mixed, working class with a few blacks. The occupational stratification and ethnic segregation in Highland Park were underscored by the influx of an exceptionally large number of young immigrant males.

When the 1910 and 1915 ratios of males to females in Highland Park (110.3/100 in 1910, and 118.3/100 in 1915) are compared to the ratios of males to females during 1910 in the United States (106/100), the state of Michigan (107.3/100), and the city of Detroit (106.6/100), the magnitude of Highland Park's truly phenomenal character is evident.

Model T Assembly: Starting engines   (From the Collections of Henry Ford Museum & Greenfield Village)

A comparison of the male to female ratio among those who are twenty-one and over at the 1910, 1915, and 1920 census reports (see Table 3.4) reveals an especially significant increase in the ratio for the decade between 1910 and 1920. With the exception of 1920, when the ratio for the Detroit region is 116 males to 100 females (see Table 3.1), the Highland Park ratio is significantly higher than that of the region. More specifically, the male to female ratios changed from 95.8 in 1910 to 124.9 in 1915, and 133.1 in 1920. By 1930 the ratio was down to 106.9, a ratio which is much closer to that of the Detroit region. Further analysis of the male to female ratio of the 1920 native white population with the 1920 total population reveals a difference that may be attributed to the large number of immigrant males in the population. The foreign-born white population was 27.2% in 1920, and the male to female ratio among those in the twenty-one and over grouping was 162.3/100. Although this ratio for Highland Park is extraordinarily high, it is consistent with the general pattern wherein "Maleness in a population has always been associated in America with areas of many foreign immigrants since migrants were disproportionately male."[33]

Table 3.6
Total Population of Highland Park, Michigan:
Number and Ratio of Males to Females over 21
by Enumeration District, 1915

District	#Males	#Females	Males/100 Females
1	772	905	85.3
2	732	756	96.8
3	985	982	100.3
4	575	667	86.2
5	902	835	108.2
6	945	674	140.2
7	1685	989	170.3
8	1799	687	262.8
9	235	210	111.9
10	280	259	108.1
11	526	524	100.3
12	624	564	110.6

Source: United States Department of Commerce. Bureau of the Census. *Special Census of the Population of Highland Park, Michigan: November 15, 1915.* Male/Female ratios computed by the author.

Table 3.7
Black Population of Highland Park, Michigan
in Twelve Enumeration Districts
by Number of Males and Females, 21 and Over, 1915

District	#Males	#Females	Males 21+	Females 21+
1	3	7	3	6
2	6	12	4	9
3	-	1	-	-
4	-	3	-	-
5	-	2	-	3
6	-	2	-	2
7	11	5	9	3
8	1	-	1	-
9	-	-	-	-
10	-	-	-	-
11	-	-	-	-
12	3	1	1	1
Total 57:	24	33	21	26

Source: Department of Commerce. Bureau of the Census. *Special Census of the Population of Highland Park, Michigan, November 15, 1915.*

Among those who were twenty-one years of age or over, the male to female ratio of Highland Park in 1915 is most startling when the population is disaggregated to enumeration districts. Specifically, and in the order of their nearness to the Crystal Palace, the ratios were 261.8, 170.3, 140.2 and 110.6 for districts 8, 7, 6 and 12 respectively. In other words, four districts near the Crystal Palace contained respectively 50.2% and 36.2% of Highland Park's males and females over twenty-one years of age; and the average male to female ratio for these districts was 173.4/100, while the overall ratio for the twenty-one and over age group was 124.9 (see Table 3.5).

The male to female ratio in the twenty-one and over black population of Highland Park in 1915 was quite different from that of the white population. To begin with, black females were more numerous than black males, and with the exception of district 7, there were more females in each district where blacks were counted. In fact (see Table 3.6), there were three districts (4, 5 and

6) where black females lived and no black males were counted; and four districts (3, 9, 10 and 11) where no blacks lived. In sum, more than 50% of the black females in this age group lived in districts where the male to female ratio favored females (85.3 and 96.8 in districts 1 and 2, respectively), and approximately 25% lived in districts where no black males lived. The statistical description of the male to female ratio of blacks living in the shadows of the Crystal Palace is no less astounding than those for whites. Together, they add up to reveal a demographic profile for Highland Park and neighboring communities that was notably different from most communities in America.

The demographic profile of Highland Park was different in at least two ways. First, although not unlike that of many towns rapidly industrializing and urbanizing, the high male to female ratio was contrary to the national trend. Secondly, not only was the male to female ratio in the opposite direction of the national pattern, but the ratio was also large when compared to most other cities in the region. While it is clear that the surplus, that is the number or proportion above a 50-50 ratio,[34] is directly related to the region's automotive industry, the consequences of the surplus of males are open to a number of interpretations. One interpretation of the presence of an excessive number of males was that they were a threat to the integrity of family life; given this interpretation, it is not surprising that the long established tradition of taking in boarders and lodgers came under attack.

Whatever the particular (local) consequences of the surplus of males (or females) for the practice of taking in lodgers and boarders, it remains clear that the demographic transition has had some important effects. Characterized by a male to female ratio that increasingly favored females, increased longevity, widening differences in the mortality of the sexes, aging populations, low fertility, etc., the demographic transition gave "rise to new circumstances between men and women that force[d] alterations in sex roles."[35] In Highland Park, these new roles were shaped in a boomtown environment.

It goes without saying that the particular demographic pattern—including the male to female ratio, the racial and ethnic mix, etc., and the boom town environment of Highland Park and the vicinity of the Crystal Palace—directly resulted from Ford's employment practices and escalating production schedules. Perhaps even more profoundly than the Detroit described by Babson, Highland Park was like prospecting towns in the Old West, "full

Model T Assembly: Testing outdoors   (From the Collections of Henry Ford Museum & Greenfield Village)

of single men living in houses and small hotels near the factories or on the city's lower East side; these bone-weary workingmen relied on the city's numerous saloons for escape from the lonely grind of factory labor."[36] Clearly, Highland Park was a boomtown stimulated by the Ford Motor Company, but urbanologists have noted that "there is a very strong cultural influence in the differential locations of men and women and that variations are not a simple function of industrialization and urbanization;"[37] nor, as Table 3.7 suggests, was it the exclusive result of any one firm in Highland Park.

In any case, regardless of the variety of cultural influences, and despite the "evils" such as those denounced by Robert W. De Forest and Lawrence Veiller,[38] there is no doubt that "any nonparental adult" in the nineteenth or twentieth century household, whether a boarder who was employed in the Crystal Palace, grandparent, spinster, aunt, or servant, "was a candidate for personal, significant relationships," and the presence of such an adult was a considerable contrast to the strict mother-father pattern in the United States since 1900."[39]

Single men (and/or perhaps married men living away from their homes) who labored in automotive plants made up a significant number of those who were candidates for the personal, significant relationships described by Warner and Fleisch. These men contributed in untold ways to shaping the culture and deciding the quality of life. In Highland Park, their wages, more often than not, were paid at the Crystal Palace (see Table 3.7).

The engineering and technical innovations that occurred in the Crystal Palace influenced the demographic transformation of the Detroit region. In response to the labor needs of a rapidly growing automotive industry, the increase in the population, the racial and ethnic mix, and the male to female ratios in the Detroit region revealed a pattern significantly different from the national trend. A few of the enumeration districts accounted for the most phenomenal aberration in Highland Park and vicinity. The enormous surplus of immigrant males and the practice of lodging and boarding in family homes (each deserving of separate investigations well beyond the scope of this study) are important to the comprehension of the social history of the cohort of workers who built the Model T and who often proudly referred to themselves as "the Ford Men."

Table 3.8
Top Ten Employers in Highland Park
Ranked by Number of Employees 1920

Name of Firm & Business	Number Employed:			
	Males	Females	Under 16	Total
Ford Motor Co./Automobiles	40,511	978	6	41,489
Maxwell Motor Co. Inc./ Automobiles	3,999	212	9	4,211
Detroit United Railway/ Car Building	531	5		536
Michigan State Telephone Co./Telephone Service	20	168		188
Detroit Creamery Co./ Milk and Cream	86	10	-	96
Ideal Box Lunch/ Lunch and Baked Goods	60	23	-	83
H.S.H. Lunch Co./ Baked Goods	42	22	-	64
Pittman's & Dean Co./ Coal and Ice	54	-	-	54
Highland Park Creamery/ Milk and Cream	48	1	-	49
Harding H.W. / Lumber	43	4	-	47

Source: Michigan Department of Labor, *Thirty-seventh Annual Report*, "Factory Inspection" by county: 286-87.

4

White- and Blue-Collar Workers
in the Crystal Palace:
Building the Model T and Forging
the New Social Order

The technological revolution in the Crystal Palace rested upon decades of progress in designing machine tools capable of producing identical interchangeable parts. First perfected in clockmaking and firearms, and greatly expanded with the bicycle craze of the 1890s, this technological revolution spread to all major manufacturing concerns and became known as the "American system of manufacture."[1] What distinguished Ford from other manufacturers and gave the company a short-lived competitive advantage was the achievement of "mass production on an unprecedented scale"—specifically that achieved with the Model T—"that required absolute standardization."[2] In the context of "Model T thinking," which evolved during the early models and was perfected during 1914, the revolution was much more than machine tools and automated assembly systems. It also involved the standardization of management, marketing, and distribution; and it resulted in the creation of a new occupational hierarchy.

Despite variations in terminology, and in some instances a lack of clarity, data reported by the Michigan Bureau of Labor Statistics for 1891 (Table 4.1), Ford's "Employees by Occupational Classification" (Table 4.2), and Zunz's stratified sample of 4,864 heads of households interviewed in the 1920 United States Census (Table 4.3) clearly demonstrate that the "new occupational hierarchy" that emerged from the technological and managerial revolution in the Ford plants consisted of three distinct classes of automotive employees.

At the top of the new occupational hierarchy at Ford and at an increasing number of other firms was a "new subspecies of economic man—the salaried manager."[3] The "subspecies" first appeared in the railroad and telegraph industries, which were the first to employ a large number of full-time managers to perform the new "economic function of administrative coordination and allocation" and the evaluation of the activities of a number of widely scattered operations.[4] This new class of employee—middle and top managers—form an entirely new breed of businessman since, "as late as 1840 there were no managers who supervised the work of other managers and in turn reported to senior executives who themselves were salaried managers."[5] It is significant that this subspecies of managers came in those industries and enterprises epitomized by the Crystal Palace, "where technology permitted several processes of production to be carried on within a single factory or works."[6] Moreover, the rate of increase in the population of this new breed of managers was directly related to the level of output per worker: "As the number of workers required for a given unit of output declined, the number of managers needed to supervise . . . increased. . . . Mass production factories became manager intensive."[7] Approximately 21.5% of all employees at the Crystal Palace in 1917, this group included salaried supervisors, engineers, accountants, clerks, inspectors, and "technicals." "At Ford," as evidenced by the experience of P.E. Martin, Charles Emil Sorensen, and a host of others, "we can see the solidification of white-collar workers into a distinct group, as well as the movement of skilled workers across the collar line to management posts."[8]

Peter Edward Martin, known as "Ed" or "Pete" among his co-workers, began with Ford in the Experimental Room of the Mack Avenue plant in 1903. By 1906 he had advanced to foreman of the Ford Motor Company and to general superintendent of production on January 13, 1919.[9] It was said that Martin was a "hard-boiled" and "quietly stern" supervisor who was "feared by all but Henry Ford himself." Martin was able to operate any machine under his supervision, was recognized as an accomplished machine designer, and is credited with helping to launch the Model T and perfecting the moving assembly system. According to one interpretation, Martin's reputation and "respect for a man's labor" led to Martin's being the only manager later permitted to enter the Rouge Plant during a bitter strike. After the infamous "Battle of the Overpass" on May 26, 1937, Walter Reuther of the United Auto Workers allowed Martin to retrieve personal papers he had left on his desk.[10] On December 24, 1924, Martin reached the top of the pyramid of Ford employees when he was appointed first vice president in charge of manufacturing.

Probably the best known of Ford's lieutenants, Charles Emil Sorensen started with the company as an experimental pattern maker in 1905 and became head of the Pattern Department in 1907. During the development of the Model T, Sorensen was assistant superintendent of production under P.E. Martin. Sorensen was instrumental in Ford's purchase of the Keim Mills factory in Buffalo, New York. Including the casting of the one-piece cylinder block Sorensen contributed several innovations to Model T production. Moreover, Sorensen noted that it is a "misconception that the final assembly line originated in our Highland Park plant in the summer of 1913. It was born then, but it was conceived in July 1908 at the Piquette Avenue plant and not with the Model T but during the last months of Model N production."[11] It was in the middle of April 1908, six weeks after public announcement of the Model T "that the idea occurred to me that assembly would be easier, simpler, and faster if we moved the chassis along, beginning at one end of the plant with a frame and adding the axles and the wheels; then moving it past the stockroom, instead of moving the stockroom to the chassis."[12] "Cast Iron Charlie," as Ford dubbed him, like P.E. Martin, was "feared by all but Henry Ford himself" and "in the plant, just the sight of him sent shivers through the average worker and was likely to be subject for discussion at the workers' supper table that evening."[13] Sorensen left the Highland Park plant in October 1915 to join the Henry Ford & Son Company in Dearborn, Michigan, where he supervised tractor production. Later, Sorensen would become the chief supervisor at the Rouge, but his "crowning achievement was the design of production layout of the mammoth Willow Run plant in Ypsilanti, Michigan, where the giant B-24 bombers were produced during World War II at the phenomenal rate of one every hour."[14]

In 1908 William S. Knudsen was general superintendent of the Keim plant in Buffalo, New York, where mufflers, gasoline tanks, fenders, and other parts for the Model T were manufactured. Ford purchased the Keim plant in January 1911, and hired its executives; in 1913, the plant equipment and sixty-two men were moved to the Crystal Palace. Knudsen was initially given charge of Ford's thirty or so branch assembly plants, and he did not arrive in Michigan until 1915, when he became production manager in the Highland Park plant. Speaking of exercising his authority as boss of production in the Crystal Palace, Knudsen said that he learned to shout "hurry up" in fifteen languages. It is said that employees worked hard for "Big Bill" who supervised the production of ambulances, trucks, aircraft motors, and was in charge of Eagle Boat production during World War I. Knudsen left the Ford Motor Company on April 1, 1921, started work for General Motors on February 12, 1922, and within three years was vice president of the Chevrolet Division. Knudsen had boarded at 122 Medbury in Detroit until his family arrived; he then purchased a house at 137 Moss Avenue, "a modest home on a pleasant street"[15] only three blocks from the Crystal Palace. In 1917 he bought ten acres in Grosse Isle, and in 1925 built on Balmoral Drive.

Beneath the elites, Martin, Sorensen, Knudsen et al., there was a small army—about six hundred in 1913—of white-collar employees who contributed mightily to the success of the Ford Motor Company. This group included men such as Clarence Willard Avery, who was a "major contributor to the techniques of mass production" and "determined the optimal rate of line speed and the distribution of workers along the line . . . and introduced time standards throughout the plant."[16] Also in this group were "technicals" such Eugene Jeno Farkas, who on October 1, 1913, was in charge of the experimental drafting room. Here also, were clerks such as Russel Hudson McCarrol whose early work "concerned problems related to car finishes, abrasives, water soluble oils, and lubricants" in 1915, and who transferred to the Rouge around 1920. Also Frank Charles Campsall, who worked in Purchasing, and Howard Woodworth Simpson, one of the few engineers in the first cohort of Ford's engineers to hold a college degree, and who worked in the tool design department. Joseph A. Galamb started with Ford on December 11, 1905, and along with Henry Ford and H.C. Wills would share the major credit for designing the Model T. In 1914 he was in charge of the Engineering Department and was designated chief engineer in 1916.

By far the largest group in the first generation of the "new occupational hierarchy" was the skilled and semi-skilled class, a total of about 64% of all workers. This class was a mixture of what was traditionally recognized as skilled workers, and "a new class of semi-skilled workers, who needed neither substantial training nor physical strength."[17] In this classification were foremen, machinists, (i.e., mechanics), assemblers, molders, painters, and a long list of specialists, including toolmakers, etc. In this group were men such as Richard Kroll, who began as a mechanic in the Experimental Department in 1905 and became head of the Inspection Department, and later head of the Quality Control Division. William F. Pioch, a machinist who joined Ford in 1912 in the tool design department headed by Karl Emde, recalled that he designed a cap to cover the universal joints. He said, "I designed the job with a special spindle that would take the part and just throw it in there, automatically clamp it, and start the machine." The net result was that "four new devices did the work of forty lathes."[18] Pioch would soon become head of the Tool Design Department in 1926, and was later chief engineer at the Willow Run bomber plant. As will be seen, it was not uncommon for tinkerers to move up into the ranks of the elites of the Ford Motor Company.

At the very bottom of the pyramid representing the "new occupational hierarchy" in the Ford Motor Company during 1917 were the 14.6% of the workers who were classified as unskilled labor. They were listed on company employment records as laborers, machine hands, autoworkers, sheet metal-workers and the like; in some instances, a lower class called unskilled service workers lists sweepers and watchmen.

Unfortunately, it is still the case that comparatively little is known about the individual lives of unskilled workers. Undoubtedly, though, these are the men at whom "[f]oremen were constantly yelling as Knudsen said he once did, 'Hurry up! Hurry up!' This English phrase haunted many an Italian or Slav immigrant in his sleep."[19] Although the sample size is insufficient for meaningful statistical analysis, the data in table 4.6 are nevertheless an accurate representation of the actual distribution of workers in the Crystal Palace in 1920. Most striking is that 57.1% of Italian workers and 31.8% of "other foreign born" were classified as unskilled labor, while there were no native Germans, German Americans, or Swiss Americans in this classification. More so than workers in the other classifications, these were the men about whom William C. Klann spoke when he said, "We were driving them of course. We were driving them in those days. . . . Ford was one of the worst shops for driving men."[20] These men maintained the lowest ranks of the army of 60,000 toilers working at the Highland Park and Rouge plants in an environment that had become largely "faceless and impersonal."

With the exception of the cutbacks in both the number of employees and the decreased level of production resulting from the effects of World War I and the recession of 1920, Table 4.4 reveals a pattern of virtually continuous growth in the number of hourly employees and the number of Model Ts produced. In addition to the workers noted in the table, there was an increasingly large percentage of executive, engineering, and office workers; in 1913 there were approximately six hundred in this class of white-collar employees. The increased levels of employment and production were accomplished by the institution of dramatic changes in ethnic diversity, skill-level, and social class composition of the workforce. Frederick Winslow Taylor's "scientific management" provided the basis of the new social relations and occupational structure. Fundamental to Taylor's system was the assertion "that management, not workers, should control the workplace." This conflicted with traditional work patterns in many industries where "skilled craftsmen supplied the technical know-how to run the workshop and management concentrated on the commercial side of the business."[21] In the Crystal Palace, a new manager class developed and assumed a dominant position in the process. But before the revolution would be consolidated, it was necessary to replace the old regime with a new set of social relations, i.e., the new occupational hierarchy.

Despite the obvious importance of the managerial revolution, much of the writing, both scholarly and the somewhat more journalistic, analyzing the evolution of the Ford Motor Company has more or less focused on the invention of automated production and assembly process, the five-dollar daily wage, and the welfare work of the Sociological Department. The particular emphases have, of course, varied in accordance with the scope of each author's particular objective. Yet, as both Olivier Zunz (*Making American Corporate*) and Alfred D. Chandler (*The Visible Hand*) have emphasized, the managerial aspect of the revolution has by-and-large been neglected by both historians and economists. For example, although Thomas C. Cochran recognized the transformation of relations in the workplace as the "basic social revolution of the twentieth century," he nevertheless "neglected the actions of middle-class middle managers in developing corporate policy" and bringing about the revolution.[22]

Sidney Glazer, for example, stated that Ford's Highland Park plant saw the inauguration of two revolutionary practices that set the pace for the expansion of the automotive industry, and thereby for the transformation of the Detroit area. The first of the revolutionary practices was the introduction of the principle of mass production and assembly, which Glazer rightfully characterized as a major technological phenomenon of this century. The second practice, the minimum five-dollar daily wage, was one that would soon revolutionize wage scales throughout the nation.[23] Similarly, in *The Car Culture*, James Flink remarked that Ford's major innovations—the movable-belt assembly line, the five-dollar daily wage, the Model T and the Fordson tractor—influenced America in the twentieth century more than the Progressive Era and the New Deal combined.[24] In part, because of the fanfare with which Ford's innovations were publicized, and perhaps because of the particular perspectives of some writers, the implementation of the continuous assembly line and the five-dollar daily wage has tended to overshadow the equally, if not more important, changes that brought a new breed of managers into the production process.

Standardization such as that in the Crystal Palace was a stratum in the multilayered organizational revolution of the late nineteenth and early twentieth century. The revolution "was not simply imposed from the top down by a corporate elite exploiting a growing labor force of immigrants, a growing army of white-collar workers, and a growing number of salaried managers." "Rather," asserted Zunz "corporate goals were simultaneously adopted and devised by an aspiring new salaried class that grew with the corporations themselves and that helped transform the larger middle-class."[25] At the center of this ever expanding middle-class was what Chandler called "the new subspecies of economic man—the salaried manager."[26]

Recently, Zunz emphasized that Alfred D. Chandler's *The Visible Hand* (1977) represents a major breakthrough in the study of the managerial revolution. "Chandler linking the growth of giant companies to that of a new managerial class, moved away from the exclusive study of financial manipulators and corporate presidents and vice-presidents," and concentrated on management in a larger sense. "He examined such issues as the creation of middle-level managers, the nature of their responsibilities, the new techniques of accounting and statistical reporting they developed, and the professionalization of their loyalties."[27] Chandler recognized that the middle-level executives, this "subspecies of economic man—the salaried manager," was a situation unlike that of the top executives; this new breed of men (and they were exclusively men) dealt with issues largely outside the purview or interests of boards of directors, they dealt with the daily routine of management.[28] "Chandler, however, told his story from an organizational stand point, without social analysis," but, with *Making America Corporate* (1990), Zunz begins the social analysis which has been largely absent from previous studies.

Unlike Chandler, "whose focus was on management, not on managers," Zunz emphasizes that "the middle-level executive is not simply a stage in an organizational flow chart, but a specific person in specific social circumstances whose degree of independence and whose part in a larger 'business' culture can be assessed." Hence, Zunz "focuses on the corporate middle-level managers who made decisions, devised standardized ways of working, and adopted new living patterns that weakened the significance of geographical boundaries within regions and reduced the de facto cultural autonomy that had characterized many communities."[29] They "played an important part in promoting a new work culture and, as an influential group, they carried the organizational revolution into key sectors of society long before competing versions of Taylorism and scientific management extended it to millions of workers."[30]

Writing in 1975 (revised 1995), Daniel Nelson is among the writers who has been especially attentive to the critical revolution in management. According to Nelson, there were three essential elements in the transformation of the Ford Motor Company: first was "a technological dynamic, as technological innovation produced, often inadvertently, fundamental changes in the factory environment and in human relationships that derived from it"; the second element was a managerial dynamic, as managers attempted to impose order and system on the manufacturing organization"; the final element, Nelson argued, was a "personnel dynamic, as managers began deliberate efforts to organize and control the factory labor force."[31] Unlike many observers, Nelson has attached a major significance to both the intellectual and the human dimensions of the managerial revolution.

Regarding the significance of the creation of a manager class, Peter F. Drucker has asserted, "Indeed, Scientific Management is all but a systematic philosophy of worker and work. Altogether it may well be the most powerful as well as the most lasting contribution America has made to Western thought since the Federalist Papers."[32] Along with Drucker, Nelson, and Chandler, the most prominent scholars of the evolution of the Ford Motor Company, including Nevins and Meyer, and somewhat less complimentary writers such as Robert W. Dunn and Keith Sward, have all recognized the significance of the managerial revolution.

In each case, although from different perspectives with different emphases, noted scholars have concerned themselves with the relationship of scientific management, or Taylorism, to increased production, to problems associated with the flood of unskilled labor, and to the consequential displacement of skilled craftsmen. Yet, despite the eloquence with which authors have analyzed Ford's implementation of scientific management, studies have often suffered for having taken a perspective that attempts to comprehend how the "Taylorized" pattern of social relations in the Crystal Palace gave control of the production processes to managers, without giving due consideration to the social and historical origins of this newly created manager class.

Harry Braverman's work *Labor and Monopoly Capital* (1974) does not focus exclusively on the Ford Motor Company, but his observations regarding scientific management and the new manager class are most enlightening. Referring to the political economy in which the social and technological revolutions within the Crystal Palace occurred, Braverman points out that the social formation of monopoly capital had its beginnings in the latter decades of the nineteenth century. "It was then that the concentration and centralization of capital, in the form of the early trusts, cartels and other forms of combination, began to assert itself,"[33] and it was then that modern capitalist industry and finance began to take shape. In an earlier chapter, "The Origins of Management," Braverman noted that, in a setting of rapidly revolutionizing technology the capitalist "brought into being a wholly new art of management, which even in its early manifestations was far more complete, self-conscious, painstaking, and calculating than anything that had gone before."[34] With respect to the insertion of the manager class into the production equation, Braverman noted, "It was not that the new arrangement was 'modern,' or 'large' or 'urban' which created the new situation, but rather the new social relations which now frame the production process," and the antagonism between the owners for whose benefit the process is carried on, those who manage, and the production workers who provide the labor."[35]

Utilizing a somewhat novel approach that analyzes narration as the instrument of change, Martha Banta has also emphasized the point that the revolutionary transformation of work, the work environment, and the workers themselves were not simply a new order imposed by barons and managers but the result of a two-way exchange. "As for the protagonists" of this revolution, "they include owners, managers, and workers; women and men; old-stock Americans, immigrants, and minorities; producers and consumers; and representatives of almost every class and caste."[36] By individuals and by members of groups, "[n]arratives were *told* to employers who wanted more productivity at less cost for the sake of greater profits as well as to workers caught up in management's experiments with quality control, which shaped both the making of products and laborer's lives. Just as compulsively, narratives were *told by* managers and workers alike in order to persuade or to dissuade, to justify or to condemn"[37]—"everyone caught up in the times had tales to tell that 'spoke' the times into being."[38]

Braverman recognized the significance of the displacement of skilled craftsmen and the appearance of increasingly large numbers of unskilled workers. But, unlike some other writers, especially Meyer and Nevins, Braverman argued that the displacement of skilled labor is deeply imbedded in the capitalist mode of production; and in accordance with Taylor's principles of scientific management, the replacement of skilled craftsmen with unskilled labor entails (indeed, depends upon) the creation of a managerial class that functions as a buffer between the antagonistic interests of the production workers and the owners. The managers became the repository of "skill" in the production process. In other words, the displacement of skilled craftsmen involved much more that merely replacing skilled labor with unskilled labor; it embodied a whole new set of social and class relations.

Labor was already socially divided when the technological revolution, and the managerial revolution, took root in the automotive industry. But the rationalization of tasks (i.e., the detailed division of labor) that subdivided human labor into its lowest common denominators (labor of the mind and labor of the hand) would not occur without a revolution in methods of assembly and production. In the context of the Ford Motor Company and the Crystal Palace, as in other industrial sites of the early decades of the twentieth century, the labor of the mind was given to the newly created, white-collar manager class, while the labor of the hand was left for the blue-collar, unskilled worker. According to Braverman's assessment, "The separation of hand and brain [was] the most decisive single step in the division of labor taken by the capitalist mode of production."[39] In the final analysis, the transfer of knowledge (i.e., skill) employed in production to managers partially fulfills the conditions of the first principle of scientific management which states that "the disassociation of the labor process from the skills of the worker," approximates "the principle of separation of conception from execution.[40]

While the distinction between managers and production workers may be symbolized by white and blue collars respectively, Braverman has cautioned that the traditional distinctions between "manual" and "white collar" labor virtually ceased to have meaning in the modern world of work.[41] Braverman continues, "It was not the color of the employee's collar, still less the mode of payment on an annual or monthly basis as distinguished from the daily or hourly wage of the manual worker, that in themselves had a determinate meaning, but rather the whole complex of social position and position in the enterprise and the labor process that these terms have symbolized."[42] As presently suggested by Braverman, and certainly as demonstrated in a variety of statistics and reports in the Ford Motor Company Archives (FMCA), the method of distinguishing between owners, managers and workers on the basis of white and blue collars, or on the basis of the manner in which one is paid, is inaccurate and misleading.

As an alternative way to make the distinction, Arne Kalleberg and Larry Griffin have distinguished between workers, managers, and employers on the basis of responses to two questions: the first question asks whether the respondent is self-employed, and the second asks whether the respondent supervises anyone as part of their job. Those who answer "yes" to both questions are employers, those who answer "no" to both questions are workers, and those who answer "no" to the first question and "yes" to the second question are managers.[43] If the workforce in the Crystal Palace during the Model T era had been asked to respond to the questions formulated by Kalleberg and Griffin, the answers would have been useful in analyzing the evolution of the manager class. In the absence of such answers, Charles Reitell's descriptive list of "important operations in the automobile industry," Olivier Zunz's sample of 1920 Detroit and Highland Park occupations, Stephen Meyer's discussion of social relations in the Highland Park plant, and a variety of statistics from Ford's records are more than sufficient to provide a reasonably good sketch of the origins and function, indeed the consolidation of the manager class.

Meyer has described the social relations of the shops and factories of the late nineteenth and early twentieth centuries. According to Meyer, present scholarship and existing fragmentary evidence suggest that the typical work relationships in the carriage and wagon shops, the small automobile factories, and the metalworking shops retained an essentially "artisan character." This is to say that, generally speaking, skilled mechanics controlled the labor process and were centrally involved in both the mental and physical aspects of the productive operations of the workshop or factory. In the pre-revolutionary environment, the skilled workers supervised unskilled laborers and/or helpers who did the physically most strenuous tasks in production. Even in the technologically advanced shops and factories, the dominant pattern of social relations was one in which the fundamental division in the workforce was between the skilled "mechanic" and the unskilled "laborers."[44] Meyer also notes that a symbolic manifestation of the social relations of the workplace may be seen in photographs of the period, which often showed skilled workers wearing white shirts and ties, while the unskilled worker is seen wearing the more conventional blue collar or traditional immigrant clothing.[45]

The social relations Meyer described are numerically illustrated in Table 4.1, which shows the proportions of mechanics, specialists, unskilled workers, and foremen in a 1891 sample of workers in Detroit's metal industries. It will be noted that in this sample, which probably typified the period, mechanics represented 39% of the workforce, while the less skilled specialists and unskilled workers represented 59% of those involved in production. The foremen, representing 2% of the production workforce, as suggested by their income and age, and as verified by the conditions of production in the metal working industries, were essentially upgraded mechanics. The major point to be made here is that while there is clearly a division of labor that may be comprehended in terms of the symbolic white and blue collars, the reality is that despite the differences in income (see Table 4.1), most of the workers were physically involved (albeit in varying degrees) in the production processes.

In contrast to the distribution of production workers shown in Table 4.1, the occupational classification of Ford's employees in January 1917 (Table 4.2) reveals a dramatic change in the workforce of the trend-setter of the automotive industry. Most important, of course, is the appearance of technical workers (13%), clerks (4.2%), and salaried supervisors (0.4%) who were not present in the 1891 sample. When those classified as foremen (6.2%) and inspectors (3.7%) who were present in the 1891 sample, are added to the former, it adds up to a manager class that was not physically involved in production; and which equals 28% of those employed. As revealed in Tables 4.1 and 4.2, a revolution in the composition of the workforce had indeed taken place.

Table 4.1
Detroit Workers in Metal Industries
by Occupational Classification 1891

Occupation	Number	Percent	*Wage	Age
Mechanics	153	39	12.58	32
Specialists	117	30	8.18	24
Unskilled	113	29	6.60	27
Foremen	9	2	19.67	38
Totals	392	100	9.95	29

Source: This is an adaptation of a table that appears in Meyer (1982); Meyer noted the sources as, "A Canvass of Agricultural Implement and Iron Working Industries in Detroit," in *Michigan Bureau of Labor and Industrial Statistics, Eighth Annual Report* (Lansing, Michigan, 1819) 1-151. The statistics reported here are the result of a computer one in ten sample of the original data (Meyer, 1982:46). Note: The wage is a weekly average.

Table 4.2
Ford Employees by Occupational Classification: January 1917

Occupation Group	Number	Percent
Specialists	22,652	55.3
Unskilled	5,986	14.6
Technical	5,391	13.2
Foremen	3,523	6.2
Clerks	1,710	4.2
Inspectors	1,533	3.7
Skilled Trades	1,003	2.4
Salaried Supervisors	198	.4
Totals	40,966	100.0

Source: Ford Motor Company Archive, Accession 940, Box 16, "List of Trades and Occupations and Number of Men Employed in Same." See also Charles Reitell, "Machinery and Its Effect Upon the Workers in the Automobile Industry," *Annals AAPS*, 116 (1924) 37-43; Meyer, 1982.

Charles Reitell, a highly respected accountant, economist and educator, wore many official hats and was exceptionally well positioned to comment authoritatively on the classification of skilled and unskilled work in the automotive industry. Reitell was a professor of economics at Elmira College (1910-1913); instructor of economics at the University of Pennsylvania (1913-1916); professor of commerce at Lawrence College in Appleton, Pennsylvania (1913-1917); economist at the National Bureau of Standards (1917-1918); professor and head of the accounting department at the University of Pittsburgh (1919-1931); and partner in the management engineers firm Stevenson, Jordan and Harrison Incorporated.[46] Among a variety of publications, "Men & Machinery" (1917), and *Machinery and Its Benefits to Labor in the Crude Iron and Steel Industries* (1917) are especially helpful in analyzing the new social order in the Crystal Palace.

In 1924 Reitell described some of the effects of the revolution: "So pronounced have been the changes that they record definite influences upon worker's wages, upon his mental actions and reactions, upon his physical being, and upon the whole social and industrial fabric of which he is a part."[47] Reitell continued by noting that within a century, inventions such as the steam engine, the cotton gin, the typewriter, the radio, the telephone and the automobile were all witnesses "of a conquering of mankind over blind nature." But, added Reitell, there was a downside to all this mechanical achievement, as workers by the millions in mills and factories were being shaped to meet the demands of these rigid machines. "The requirements of dexterity, alertness, watchfulness, rhythmic and monotonous activities, coupled with a lessening of much of the older physical requirements, are registering results that portray a new type of worker in industry."[48] In more recent times, Stephen Meyer has reiterated Reitell's concerns.

Meyer maintains that the new industrial technology that had become a reality in the Crystal Palace, "was a mixed social blessing, and perhaps even a curse which promised a material cornucopia for all," while exacting incredible social costs. Following the implementation of the new technology, "The world of work would never be the same again . . . the worker's daily routine became more monotonous and more repetitive. It dramatically altered the social structure of the shop, the factory and, in fact modern industrial society. . . . Indeed, the new industrial technology had a profound impact on modern social existence."[49]

Nowhere were the results more evident than in Highland Park, in the shadows of the Crystal Palace.

Meyer noted three areas in which Ford's new industrial technology, a technology coinciding in some ways with the fulfillment of the four principles of scientific management, had a dramatic impact on the character of work and social relations in the Crystal Palace, as well as in other firms. First, the new technology transformed the tasks and routines in the various shops and departments of the of the Crystal Palace, so that the "traditional notion of skill was completely removed form the tasks and routines of the workman." Second, a new system of workplace stratification and new patterns of social relationships emerged as the "deskilled specialist" became the principal occupational group, and foremen, subforemen, straw bosses, clerks, and inspectors increased in numbers. Finally, the new technology brought with it a new method for the control of the deskilled specialist. "The design of machines, the arrangement of men and machines, the new forms of record keeping and inspection, and the new means of mechanical conveyance all controlled the pace, the intensity, and the quality of production."[50]

In 1924 Reitell noted that changes in how the automobile was produced added to the existing confusion associated with terms such as "skilled, semi-skilled and unskilled workers."[51] More recently, further confusion has been added by the use of terms like "deskilled" and "deskilling."[52] While such terms are intuitively appealing and represent a certain reality, they are nevertheless ahistorical and, unfortunately, detract from the understanding of the most profound change in workplace stratification: the insertion of the manager class. Fortunately, Reitell outlined a useful alternative to such phrases.

Reitell wrote that "in lieu of unskilled, semiskilled and skilled there now exist tenders who operate machines, the technical force who design, plan, schedule, route and cost the work, the clerks, inspectors and foremen who record all the miscellaneous activities of the shop, check the quality and quantity of production and keep watch on the flow of materials."[53] However, according to Reitell's observations, the important operations in the automobile industry could be reduced to six primary groups, which he listed as 1) machine tenders, 2) assemblers, 3) skilled workers (i.e., those who have a trade), 4) inspectors and testers, 5) helpers, and 6) laborers.[54] Reitell added that in the eleven years between 1912 and 1923 groups 1 and 2 grew to represent a larger proportion of the total workforce.[55] Reitell's classification is invaluable, but with the exception of inspectors and testers included in group 4, the manager class is excluded. Table 4.3 complements Reitell's classification scheme.

Table 4.3 is based on a stratified sample of 4,864 heads of household counted in the 1920 United States Census, and is a valuable supplement to Reitell's classification of workers. When summarized, the table reveals that 73 workers in the sample were classified as white collar, 555 as skilled and semi-skilled, and 230 as unskilled workers. Considered along with Reitell's classification of workers involved in the "important operations in automobile production," it is noted that only inspectors and testers (group 4) may be categorized as white-collar workers; moreover, it will be observed that the number of inspectors (42/864) is consistent with Reitell's assertion that this group of workers included about 5% of the total. Together, Tables 4.1, 4.2, and 4.3 and Reitell's classification of automotive workers reveal a change from the hierarchy that was evident in the 1891 sample.

Table 4.3
Automotive Industry Occupations
by Skill Classification and Number Employed, Detroit 1920

Classification	Occupation	Number
White collar	Inspector	42
	Accountant	10
	Salesman	9
	Engineer	6
	Stock Clerk	6
Skilled and semi-skilled	Machinist	195
	Foremen	66
	Toolmaker	53
	Painter	29
	Assembler	27
	Carpenter	18
	Millwright	18
	Mechanic	17
	Trimmer	17
	Repairman	16

	Electrician	12
	Woodworker	11
	Bricklayer	11
	Auto body builder	10
	Auto body maker	9
	Finisher	9
	Steamfitter	9
	Grinder	9
	Molder	8
	Blacksmith	6
	Motor Assembler	5
Unskilled labor	Laborer	184
	Machine hand	22
	Auto worker	12
	Sheet metal worker	12
Unskilled service worker	Watchman	6

Source: This table is based on data that appears in Zunz, *The Changing Face of Inequality*, "Table A 3.2"; Zunz's table is based on a stratified sample of 4,864 heads of household who were counted in the 1920 United States Census.

Table 4.4
Number of Hourly Employees 1911-1933 and
Number of Model Ts Produced 1908-1927

Year	Number of Employees	Model Ts Produced
1908	——	309
1909	——	13,852
1910	——	23,739
1911	3,488	54,000
1912	5,710	82,000
1913	13,198	199,100
1914	14,000	240,700
1915	18,028	372,251
1916	31,298	586,203
1917	35,246	834,663
1918	32,531	382,247

1919	43,080	828,545
1920	49,337	1,038,448
1921	31,745	939,652
1922	44,194	1,315,000
1923	63,168	2,055,300
1924	61,759	1,991,532
1925	50,565	1,605,534
1926	41,326	1,631,299
1927	31,051	385,679
1928	33,125	——
1929	13,444	——
1930	3,611	——
1931	1,840	——
1932	780	——
1933	524	——

Source: The employment statistics for the years 1911, 1912 and 1913 were taken from Ford Motor Company Archive, Accession 6, Box 31, and 1914 from Meyer's *Five Dollar Day*. The remaining employment figures were extracted from Nevins's *Ford: The Times, the Man, the Company*; the source was given as the Ford Motor Company Industrial Relations Analysis Department. The source for Model T production is Ford Motor Company Archive, Accession 922, "Model T Production Statistics."

Among the many changes wrought in the new factory system pioneered by Ford, the displacement of the foreman by the manager class was perhaps the most profoundly important. Prior to the advent to the new system, which has been described by one writer as "Fordism,"[56] it was common for manufacturers to entrust most aspects of the day-to-day operations to foremen, first-line supervisors.[57] Typically, "the technicians, clerks and other staff specialists . . . who dominate the present-day manufacturing plant were unknown in the late nineteenth century factory." Clearly, "before 1900 and in most factories before 1920, the foreman was the undisputed ruler of his department, gang, crew or shop."[58] The foreman's status and authority, which were usually achieved through the acquisition of a "skill," were based upon several important functions he performed. First, and most important, he "got the work out"; a job that varied according to the degree of management participation in production decisions. A second function was to interpret the management's policies to the workers. The third function consisted of hiring, training, motivating, and disciplining workers.[59] Although nineteenth-century managers and foremen seldom distinguished the three activities from "getting the work out" and enforcing the employer's rules, in the new system the foreman's personnel function became the responsibility of "expert" managers. While firms gradually reduced the foreman's power to recruit and train the factory labor force, they also added new personnel programs outside the foreman's jurisdiction that ultimately reinforced the trend toward centralized control over employee recruitment and training;[60] and in the case of the Ford Motor Company in the Crystal Palace, eventually extended that control into the homes of the workers.

As the internal authority structure of the Ford Motor Company was being restructured and as skilled workers and foremen were displaced by the manager class, there was also a significant change in the size and ethnic composition of the workforce (see Table 4.5). Generally speaking, it would be accurate to conclude that the ethnic composition in the Crystal Palace was merely a reflection of the ethnic makeup of the region as a whole. Richard Lee, who headed Ford's first Personnel Department and who preceded Samuel Marquis as head of the Sociological Department, noted the significance of foreign-born employees. Lee stated that, among those employed in the Highland Park plant, there were fifty known nationalities and one unknown; more specifically, he noted that "Out of the [8,000] men working here, there are 73 that did not know what they were, 1,829 Americans, 1,812 Poles, 1,465 Russians, 522 Roumanians, 366 Germans and 137 Servians [sic]." "So," continued Lee, "you can see, the foreign element predominates,"[61] in the Crystal Palace. Lee's assessment is borne out in table 4.5.

Table 4.5 further supports the assertion that the "foreign element" was prominent: here it is shown that in January 1916, while most of the employees at the Crystal Palace were "American," Polish, Canadian, Italian, Roumanian, and German workers (along with fifty other nationalities, each with less than one hundred employed), were significant among the total number of employees. Since the Roman Catholic religion is often included as an ethnic characteristic of the foreign workers who came to the Detroit area during the late nineteenth and early twentieth centuries, the fact that 13,586 employees at the Crystal Palace were designated as Roman Catholic also attests to the prominence of the "foreign element."

It goes without saying, of course, that although the ethnics were numerically prominent, they were not proportionately distributed throughout the workforce. One Ford Motor Company official (c.1914) noted that while the percentage of foreign people who came to work as laborers in the Highland Park plant was rather high, they were of various "types." More precisely, continued the official:

You see, in the machine lines, I would say they were more or less Americans or they were maybe of German descent or people of that *type*, you know. More skilled help was naturally the American *type*, but we did secure a lot of Austrians and Germans, you know, good die makers, you know. I would say the highest percentage was an American *type*.

In the lower classifications, such as press operators or grinders or laborers, well, we had the foundry here, foundry help. In the beginning it was a lot of Russian, Polish, Croation, Austrian, people of that *type*. We didn't have any Negroes until W.W. I. That was the beginning of the migration of the colored people in Detroit.[62]

Table 4.5
Nationalities and Religions of Ford's Crystal Palace Employees in January 1916 by Numerical Prominence

Nationality	Number
American	12,328
Polish	5,280
Canadian	1,392
Italian	1,197
Roumanian	1,002
German	1,001
*	*
Religion	
Roman Catholic	13,586
Protestant	12,427
Greek Catholic	1,660
Jewish	995

Source: Ford Motor Company Archives, Dearborn Michigan, Accession 62, Box 59.

Table 4.6
Occupational Status of Highland Park Automotive Workers
by Ethnic Group and Occupational Classification

Ethnic Group & Number	Occupational Classification			
	White Collar	Skilled and Semi-skilled	Unskilled *(wl)	(sw)
Native White American/80	32.5	42.5	6.3	6.3
British/17	17.6	47.1	29.4	—
Canadian:				
English/13	23.1	46.2	15.4	7.7
American/13	30.8	38.5	15.4	—
British Am	—	25.0	—	25.0
German Am/9	11.1	66.7	—	—
British Am/7	42.9	14.3	14.3	14.3
Italian/7	—	28.6	57.1	14.3
Armenian/6	—	33.3	16.7	16.7
Irish Am/3	—	66.7	—	—
Swiss Am/3	66.7	33.3	—	—
German/2	—	—	—	—
Other foreign-born/22	22.7	31.8	31.8	4.5
Other native-born/5	20.0	40.0	20.0	—
Totals:/164	49	77	27	11
Percent	25.7	40.	14.1	5.8

Source: This table is based on "Table 13.5" in Zunz, *The Changing Face of Inequality*, 358-59. Zunz's statistics are derived from the 1920 United States Census, and represent the results of an equal probability sample of heads of households in Highland Park. [Note: (wl) and (sw) respectively, designate wage labor and service worker.

The Ford official's assessment of the proportion of the various "types" of workers employed in the Crystal Palace, and the particular classes of jobs that they held, is confirmed in the 1920 United States Census report, which included statistics on job classification by nationality.

According to Zunz's analysis of a sample of the 1920 data, the "American type" occupied the white collar, skilled and semi-skilled positions in the hierarchy of Highland Park's workforce, while the "lower classification" was reserved for the Polish, Croatian, Italian, and other "people of that type." In short, the testimony of Ford officials, combined with the statistics recorded in Table 4.6, strongly suggests that virtually all of the manager class would come from the ranks of the "American type." In some ways, the bias in favor of the "American type" is a multifaceted irony.

It must have seemed a paradox to Frederick Winslow Taylor that in "creating" scientific management, he essentially destroyed the opportunities of future engineers to have real apprenticeships with engineering masters. During his later life Taylor, as Robert Kanigel puts it, "would look back wistfully to those days at the pump works," and "he'd tell anyone who'd listen that no engineering graduate should leave school without a year in a shop" such as the Midvale Iron Works. Although "the father of scientific management" believed every engineer should have such an apprentice experience, his systems of industrial efficiency ironically helped make that impossible.[63]

At another level, the bias in Taylor's science is ironic in two respects. In discussions regarding the displacement of the artisan class, the artisan is usually portrayed as the victim of the villainous "unskilled" immigrant worker whose lowly habits allowed him to live on lower wages than those required by the artisan. Since it was rational to employ labor at the cheaper rate, it is generally surmised that the artisan was replaced by the immigrant. However, the present analysis strongly suggests that the foregoing scenario is ahistorical, inaccurate, and incomplete. It would be more correct to argue that while the artisan was replaced, he was not replaced by the immigrant, but by the manager-class, almost none of whom were of the immigrant type. Secondly, the bias is ironic in that, while it is often recognized that Taylor's scientific principles may have been the foundation of social stratification in the Crystal Palace and other plants, there is only silence on the question, How scientific was the selection of the manager-class?

5

From Ethnic Squalor to White-Collar Splendor: Some Observations on the Quality of Life of the Model T Cohort, 1910-1927

In addition to the new manufacturing and managerial technology adopted in the production of the Model T, the demographic transformation of the region was also a factor in determining the quality of life experienced in communities such as Highland Park and Hamtramck, which literally lay within the shadows of the Crystal Palace. The demographic transformation involved a tremendous increase in the size of the total population of the region, a change in the racial and ethnic mix of the population, a change in the ratio of children to adults, and a change in the ratio of males to females. These changes, along with the new manufacturing and managerial technology, contributed greatly to defining the quality of life in the region. Following the Environmental Protection Agency definitions and prescriptions concerning the study of the quality of life, and focusing on 1) home and housing conditions, 2) employment and income, 3) health, and 4) political power, this chapter examines the quality of housing occupied by the various classes[1] in Detroit and in the vicinity of the Crystal Palace.[2]

Private citizens and public officials alike were well aware of the existence of densely populated neighborhoods in the city of Detroit, and that there was (and continues to be) a close correlation of living "conditions" with fertility and mortality, and with the frequency and severity of diseases such as tuberculosis. It was with this knowledge that investigators fanned out across Detroit to make a record of such "abominable conditions." As reported in the *Detroit Free Press* in June of 1907, in seeking such overcrowded conditions the investigator "naturally" first turns his steps in the direction of the foreign quarter. In one house of modest size, investigators found fourteen children, aside from a considerable number who had reached the age where they were engaged in the daily struggle for existence. In another house twelve children ranging in age from babes in arms up to ten years "after which the boys are armed with baskets of fruit and sent forth or accompany their elders with pushcarts about the city." Just a few doors from Larned Street, forty-seven men were found residing in a house of "modest proportions."[3]

When investigators arrived unannounced at the "cottage" on the upper east side of Detroit they were greeted by a heavy-set woman wearing, "so far as the casual observer could judge . . . a coarse woolen undershirt of male persuasion, a faded blue calico skirt, a coat of grime and a smile."[4] Acting as if the investigators were perspective boarders, Magdalene showed them two attic rooms. The first room was reserved for the landlady. The second room was about twenty feet deep and high enough for a man of ordinary height to stand without coming in contact with the rafters. In this room there were "five beds whose condition beggared description. Some were cots. Others were iron bedsteads of uncertain age. . . . The greasy mattresses, the grimy woolen blankets, the absence, as a rule of anything even suggestive of linen" presented a scene the investigator found almost unbelievable. On the ground floor the investigators were shown four small rooms with thirteen double beds, all in the same condition as those which filled the attic. "Some were occupied, others were vacant; for be it known that double shifts in the matter of sleeping accommodations are worked by many of the thrifty managers of these foreign boarding houses, one set of roomers, or more strictly speaking, 'bedders,' piling out and going to work, while another crew . . . climbs into the still warm beds and are soon lost in slumber."[5] A tiny room at the rear of the house serves as the kitchen, here one of the "bedders" stood at a small table "alternately slicing cabbage, onions and liver into a huge stew pan, for the noon hour was approaching, and the hungry hordes would soon come trooping in from the nearby car shops for their midday repast of stew and rye bread."[6]

Each "bedder" paid monthly the sum of $3, this amount covering bed, washing, and cooking. "In return the landlady does all the marketing, prepares the meals, keeps the house in shape, makes those eighteen beds whenever they are unoccupied long enough and washes those heavy undershirts two or three times a week." Magdalene buys all the provisions, and each day the table expenses are divided pro rata among the "bedders," she being allowed her board in addition to what she receives from each man.[7]

On Riopelle Street, a short block from Magdalene's property, the investigators entered a house that they called "deplorable." Here ten beds were crowded into four small rooms. "In one of these rooms, occupied by three beds, three men and two women sat grouped about on the edges of the beds." The "cellar bottom was covered with six inches of water that had backed up from the sewer and which gave an unbearable stench." In the few square feet that was recognized as a "back yard," the investigators found a "rough shack," about eight feet wide and sixteen feet long, that had one door and no windows; in this shack "five cot-beds are arranged— and each of these beds is occupied nightly by at least one man, sometimes two." In this backyard was "a collection of refuse of every sort, covered with a slimy deposit, the drainage of dirty wash water, that should result in the place being condemned."[8]

The squalid conditions encountered at Magdalene's boarding house, and those observed on Riopelle Street were typical of those found in many neighborhoods. For example, on Roby Street in the Milwaukee Junction district there was one two-story frame structure, about the size of an ordinary house, that was divided into eight three-room "apartments." The average rent for each was $7.50 a month. In one of these three-room apartments there were five double beds. A similar condition was found on Hastings street, where overcrowding was the rule rather than the exception. In "Little Sicily" located at East Congress and Larned Streets, tumbledown houses teeming with inhabitants brought in hefty profits. Atwater and Franklin Streets had their Syrian colony. "Little Hungary" in old Delray had "boarding houses presided over by swarthy Amazons that would contribute a good start, numerically, toward populating a village." Generally speaking, these settlements had "problems but a trifle less serious than those arising among the same classes in the northeastern part of the city, and there were other localities too numerous to mention."[9] Investigators emphatically stated that these conditions were not exceptional cases; rather, they were typical of others found in many districts in Detroit's foreign quarters.

Although it was difficult to determine with any great precision which neighborhood was the most densely populated, it was believed that nowhere were there more persons than were contained in the two blocks on Larned Street east, between Brush and Antoine—the heart of the Italian quarter. Closely following the Italians were the Hungarians in old Delray, a portion of the Eighteenth ward. "There are other sections of the city where families are huddled together, but the congestion is not so great as in the instances cited. Nor is there to be noted at any point the abject poverty usually accompaniment of overcrowded quarters." It might not measure up to American standards, but according to investigators in 1907 "there is little want and less vice."[10]

Investigators found that densely populated Polish enclaves had a somewhat different practice with regard to using the land. According to the *Free Press,* "Your Pole is a thrifty mortal also" and "To him the waste of land to be seen on every side is little short of criminal." The community in the vicinity of Hastings Street and Garfield Avenue furnished some interesting illustrations of their exceptional residential pattern. "One entire alley in a single block just off Hastings Street is lined with houses teeming with people. Block after block the eye is greeted by nothing but long rows of closely built cottages, the style of architecture seldom varying. . . . The same conditions are encountered on the west side of the city where is another Polish settlement of several thousand persons."[11]

In comparison to residents in the Polish neighborhood at Hastings Street and Garfield Avenue, immigrants such as Felek and Teklunia Koscielski lived a "life of luxury." At age nineteen Felek Koscielski was living in Russian-dominated Poland, where he was suspected of being a member of a Polish underground organization (Polska Partia Socjalisyczna). Although he was not a member of this underground organization, his family feared for his safety and arranged a pass for him to "visit" an aunt in Austrian Poland. Felek did not return to Poland; instead he came to America around 1910-1912. Teklunia, the eldest of six children under the care of a widowed mother, balked at an arranged marriage and "one morning she started off, presumably to her daily chore of milking the cow, left the milk cans behind the stable door, and walked out of the village to meet some friends who were leaving for America."[12] Although the two did not travel the same path—one landed in New York and the other in Montreal—their experiences were comparable. They began their lives in America "living in boarding houses, looking for work, working harder than they ever had to in Europe, making foolish mistakes, being insulted ('Polander' was the prevalent term of derision), being misunderstood because of the language barrier . . . Eventually, both came to Detroit, met and married."[13]

Before marriage, Teklunia worked as a dishwasher in a restaurant where "she burned her hands because she made the water too hot. She was so determined that those dishes would be really clean."[14] Felek began work in the "factory" in the pre-union days. Felek frequently complained about his foremen and company policies, but he was proud of his contribution to the auto industry. When he saw a Cadillac on the road, he would say: "There! My work is on that Cadillac. Every fender of every Cadillac is welded by me." The pay checks bought and maintained a home in a Polish neighborhood where they had a garden with carrots, parsley, onions, beets, and tomatoes, to be eaten in season and canned and stored for the winter. There was a lawn, neatly trimmed and weeded, and flowers of many different varieties for continuous bloom and for trading with the neighbors.[15] The quality of housing for Magdalene Marachal and her "bedders" was inferior to that of the Koscielskis, and it was even more inferior to that of Ford's elite. However, it was better than the housing available to black workers.

For the vast majority of Black Detroit, without respect for occupation and social class, the housing situation was abominable. Consider, for example, a house on St. Antoine Street, just off Adams, which was occupied by fifteen regular tenants and a varying number of transients. This place had six rooms, no toilet or bath, and rented for $75.00 a month. The people were all black and were living in Detroit's black ghetto already filled to bursting.[16]

George Edmund Haynes, a trained sociologist and contemporary of the Model T era, offered an assessment of the housing conditions based largely on a sample of 407 households. Haynes argued that housing was the most pressing problem of Detroit's black newcomers, observing, "Houses for families involve not only the question of physical shelter but the problems of sanitary and moral environment."[17] The housing problem was characterized by shortages that resulted in overcrowding and excessive rents; moreover, much of the available housing was unfit for human habitation, while restrictive property covenants and racial discrimination prevented blacks from moving into more suitable environments.

There has been a great deal of commentary about the housing problem that plagued Detroit from 1900 to 1930. David Allan Levine, citing Forrester B. Washington, first head of the Detroit branch of the Urban League, observed that early contingents of the great migration immediately consumed all available housing, and there was not a vacant house or tenement in the black section of the city, where three or four families were not crowded into nearly every apartment.[18] In one shocking case, "Fourteen people lived in the attic of a house on Napoleon Street." Generally speaking, crowded conditions were made worse because "housing with no indoor bathroom facilities, no electric lights, and leaking water pipes was commonplace."[19]

David M. Katzman stated that even before the great migration housing for blacks left much to be desired.[20] In describing alley-dwelling, Katzman remarked, "Neither the alleys nor the dwellings in them were well suited for human habitation." Former sheds and stables had been converted into housing for one, two, or three families, while in 1911, the alleys were still being used as a garbage dump and posed serious health hazards. Moreover, the short supply of housing contributed to excessive rents paid by black occupants: "In 1911 an alley house between Hastings and Rivard, occupied by two families and as many boarders and lodgers as they could secure, rented for $18 month." Circumstances such as these were commonly found throughout the area. A few blocks away, in another alley community or "shanty town," houses "built of rough boards in the chicken coop style or architecture" rented for $10 a month. The disparity in the monthly rental rates paid by blacks may be seen when those rates are contrasted with rates paid in the working-class neighborhoods of 1910, where "older six-room dwellings fully serviced by utilities rented for $10 to $12 monthly, and new dwellings rented for $18 to $22."[21]

Haynes was persistent in noting that the so-called lodger evil was among the greatest problems caused by the housing shortage. He emphasized that many families living in one to four rooms were accommodating lodgers, and he noted that practically all families recorded as living in five or more rooms were taking in lodgers, while all families living in seven or more rooms had at least two lodgers. "In fact," Haynes continued, "many homes of this size were run either as rooming houses for profit or because the necessity of paying the high rents" had turned them into rooming houses.[22] Continuing his observations on the "pressing problem" of the lodger evil, Haynes noted that, "There were 7 families living in one room keeping lodgers; 146 families were living in 2 or more rooms keeping lodgers; only 100 families were reported as having no lodgers, and 98 were doubtful or unknown. Here we have a pressure against wholesome family life which is serious in the extreme."[23] The housing problems refused to go away. The housing situation for blacks was so bad in the summer of 1919 that some men, with money in their pockets, were forced to sleep in parks, and others slept in cars and on pool tables.[24] While a survey of 1,000 families showed that over half of these families took in lodgers (usually single men), the mayor's Inter-Racial Committee reported that "sanitary dwellings at a reasonable rent" were still "the exception," and there were no reasonably priced workingmen's clubs or hotels for black workers in Detroit."[25]

Black "alley dwellers" occupied an area consisting of several blocks bounded by Beaubien and Hastings on the east and west, and Napoleon and Brewster on the north. During 1911, in the rear of a Beaubien Street lot stood an old shack, measuring about fifteen by thirty feet. It had two levels, with the lower part used as a shed and stable and the upper part intended for storage of hay. The lower part remained a shed, but the hay loft had been converted into a dwelling, partitioned off with rough lumber to make two rooms and two recesses. In this rookery were housed five persons—a man, a woman, a young girl, and two adult lodgers. The windows looked out onto an alley where refuse collected through the winter. At the entrance of the building was a large box of manure that had been thrown out of an adjacent stable.

A similar shack stood in an alley between Alfred and Brewster Streets. Built of rough boards and resembling a chicken coop, it was divided into four rooms housing two families. Each paid $5 a month rent. The total value of the shack could not have been more than $25. Another alley shed between Hastings and Rivard Streets, occupied by two families and a varying number of lodgers, paid its owner rental of $18 a month. The families had long since given up trying to keep out the filth.[26]

According to Haynes, "One observer said he had seen rooms occupied by two people where the most convenient way to dress was to stand in the middle of the bed."[27] Haynes qualified his statement by indicating that the observer was probably exaggerating, but asserted that it was nevertheless "true that many buildings are very badly overcrowded and are nothing more than dilapidated shacks."

Reporting data provided by the Detroit Urban League, Haynes stated that the usual size of houses or apartments was three, four, or five rooms, and that many of them were in the midst of saloons, gambling places or "buffet flats," which were understood to be a "sort of high-class combination of a gambling parlor, a 'blind tiger,' and an apartment of prostitution," which generally operated under police protection.[28] Haynes's observations regarding the housing conditions commonly experienced by blacks were confirmed by a number of public agencies.

On the basis of a 1916 study evaluating 96 working class homes, the Detroit Board of Health found 1,974 persons occupying homes that were judged to have a capacity for not more than 1,477 persons. Moreover, it was found that only 11 of the 96 homes were judged to have sanitary bed conditions and less than 20 of the homes were in compliance with plumbing codes.[29] Despite the frenzy of housing construction, the housing shortage persisted. A survey conducted in 1919 showed that there was a shortage of approximately 33,000 housing units and that 165,000 persons were living in substandard housing.[30]

Between 1923 and 1928, over 50,000 housing units were built in the Detroit area, but this spurt of construction was not enough to meet the demand.[31] Levine noted that "housing was constructed

Table 5.1
Number of Rooms Occupied, Family Size, and Rents Paid:
A Sample of 407 Detroit Heads of Household 1918

Rooms Occupied	Family Size	Rents Paid
71-5	169-2	57 @ $15-$19
63-1	108-3	45 @ $35-$39
50-nd	51-4	43 @ $20-$24
44-6	28-5	39 @ $29-$29
43-7	19-6	29 @ $30-$34
35-4	18-1	27 @ $10-$11*
34-3	10-7	21 @ $40-$44
24-2	3-8	13 @ $45-$54
16-12	1-9	4 @ > $60
16-10		3 @ < $10
14-9		
13-8		

Source: Haynes, *Negro Newcomers in Detroit*, 1-24. (Note: nd=no data; *= one room households)

for 16,689 families in 1922; for 23,153 families in 1923; for 26,377 in 1924; for 26,679 in 1925; and for 17,287 in 1926."[32] Yet the demand by far outstripped supply. On the basis of its own investigation in 1921, the Americanization Committee of Detroit reported that many "Negroes" were living in shacks that were not fit for human habitation, for which they were paying exorbitant rents.[33] The housing situation outlined here is precisely the environment encountered by Ossian Sweet, and which he sought to avoid by moving his family into the house at 2905 Garlund Avenue.

Ossian Sweet (pronounced "ocean)[34] was born in Barstow, Florida, in the late 1890s, the eldest of ten children born to a household headed by a Methodist preacher. As a young boy, Sweet witnessed an event that would have a deep and lasting effect on him, and on those with whom he came in contact. One day he saw a mob consisting of what appeared to be thousands of white people driving a young black boy down a road near the Sweet home. While hiding himself, Sweet saw the mob pour kerosene on the boy and set fire to his flesh. He heard the boy's tortured screams pierce the air; after a while, when the crusty body no longer cried out, he listened to the gleefully triumphant howls of the drunken mob as they celebrated their work. "He saw them laughingly take photographs of the scene and then watched in horror as dozens of whites pulled souvenirs of bones and flesh off the charred remains."[35]

Sweet left home when he was twelve years old and worked at numerous jobs, including bellboy, waiter on steamships and in hotels, Pullman-porter, and janitor before attending Wilberforce University in Ohio and medical school at Howard University in Washington, D.C. By 1925, Ossian Sweet was "a young man barely in his thirties, married, with an infant daughter, he was a physician and surgeon, and specialized in gynecology," living in the city of Detroit. Sweet, like the vast majority of black Detroiters, never lived in Highland Park and never worked in the Crystal Palace. But despite his "professional status," Sweet did have much in common with the average black Detroiter. The few blacks living in Highland Park and working in the Crystal Palace had much in common with the larger community of black Detroit.

During the summer of 1925 whites in various parts of the city, as they had in years before, succeeded in preventing blacks from moving into their neighborhoods. Generally speaking, whites tried to keep blacks in place by means of loosely organized urban terrorism. As early as 1919, bombing and mob threats had succeeded in discouraging blacks from moving out of the black ghetto and into white neighborhoods, and by 1925 when the Sweet family went on trial for murder, the Ku Klux Klan was well established in Detroit and had shown its strength by nearly electing their write-in candidate (Charles Bowles) as the new mayor.[36] The Sweets knew that there would be opposition, such as that represented by the Ku Klux Klan, to their moving out of the black ghetto.

Sweet knew that his family would not be welcomed to the neighborhood where he paid a hard-earned $3,000 deposit on the $18,500 house at 2905 Garlund Avenue, near Charlevoix. In fact, expecting trouble and doubting that police protection would be forthcoming,[37] the Sweets armed themselves "with seven revolvers and automatic pistols, two rifles, a shotgun, and about 400 rounds of ammunition."[39] Having informed the police department of his intentions, on Tuesday morning September 8, 1925, the Sweet household moved into their home at 2905 Garlund Avenue.

Except for the constant parade of people who passed the house and the policemen who were on the scene all day to keep people moving, the Sweet family's first day in the new home was relatively uneventful. At midnight, 500 to 800 people still stood outside the house, but by three o'clock in the morning, the crowd had begun to dissipate and by daybreak everyone had scattered.[39]

The morning of the second day was "normal," but by late afternoon large crowds of people had gathered near the house. Apparently startled at seeing the horde milling about outside, someone in the house sang out, "My God, look at the people!"[40] Some of the mob began to throw stones at the house, some shouted curses, while seventeen policemen stood within fifty feet of the house and did nothing to dissuade them.[41] Meanwhile, Ossian Sweet turned out the lights, grabbed a gun, and ran upstairs. Some of the members of the household had not yet returned to the house from their normal daily routines, and as they drove up in a taxi and then ran toward the front of the house, they were pelted with bricks, stones, rocks and coal, as their assailants yelled "Niggers! Niggers! They're niggers. Get Them! Get the niggers!"[42] Windows were shattered. Soon, shots came from within the house.[43] Police reinforcement arrived and the Sweets were arrested.

One of the Detroit newspapers reported the aftermath in the following way: "Downtown on lower Beaubien in the huge new police building of which official Detroit was so proud, the prisoners were told that a man named Leon Breimer had been killed and another, Erik Houberg, severely wounded."[44] It was the police chief who asked the first question of Ossian Sweet: "Doctor, what business do you have moving into a white neighborhood where you are not wanted?"[45]

Ossian Sweet and the other 80,000 (approximately) immigrants arriving in Detroit in 1914-1925 enriched the city and multiplied the prospects for an improved quality of life for the immigrants themselves, as well as for the elite class of blacks who had come before them. Yet in spite of the possibilities of change for the better, "the structure—economic, social, and political—that proscribes black life [had] remained the same."[46] Katzman noted that, as illustrated in his work on Detroit, and as seen in the work of Allen Spear on Chicago, and in the work of Gilbert Osofsky on New York,[47] "there is a tragic sameness in the lives of black people today and the past," and when compared with other groups, "no group had changed so little in more than half a century."[48] With specific reference to the ways in which backward development, and everything it implies, was reflected in residential segregation, Zunz recognized the anachronistic character of black Detroit.[49]

Zunz recalled that Louis Wirth, writing in the 1920s, led the way in developing the revolutionary analytic model of residential succession in which it was assumed that blacks—the last group to enter the city—needed only to wait their turn to receive the "well-earned fruits of the toil."[50] Wirth's model offered an optimistic projection that was not confirmed by the realities of Detroit. In fact, as Zunz has put it, "blacks lived history in reverse."[51] While most ethnic neighborhoods flourished as cross-class communities providing a variety of opportunities for an improved quality of life for its members, blacks were "atomized and dispersed." The cross-class communities were transformed by the emergence of a large industrial working class. As ethnic bonds were being replaced by occupational bonds, and as upwardly mobile residents moved up in class, they left behind the communities that had nurtured them, while most urbanized "blacks were drawn into an ever growing ghetto, irrespective of their social status." The contradiction of the growth of the black ghetto was an anachronism contrasting sharply with the white ethnic groups that became more and more segmented along class lines in many sections of the metropolitan area.[52]

For Ossian Sweet and the black community whose aspirations he symbolized, the lack of political power meant that there was no protection. It meant that blacks, without regard for income and professional status, were forced to remain in the ghetto while other immigrants improved the quality of their lives by moving out of substandard housing overflowing with lodgers, and into better homes and better neighborhoods, away from the "lodger evil."

Even during the best of times, as one authority noted, "The black community in Detroit has [always] struggled to increase and sustain its overall quality of life."[53] Blacks huddled in Detroit's near eastside ghetto were plagued by "tough jobs, scarce housing and poor health."[54] Citing the United States Department of Commerce publication, "Mortality Statistics: Thirty-First Annual Report: 1930," and Ulysses W. Boykin, *A Handbook on The Detroit Negro*, Thomas commented on the relatively severe health hazards faced by blacks in Detroit.[55] Given what is commonly known about the relationship of home and housing conditions, occupation, and the quality of health, the picture drawn by Thomas, while not clearly discernible in the data found in the Ford Motor Company Archives, is not inconsistent with the fragments of evidence that describe the experience of the comparatively small number of black workers who were employed in the Crystal Palace.

Thomas reported that during the peak years of black immigration to the Detroit area (c.1915-1920), while the death rate of whites remained constant at 12.8 per 1,000, the death rate among blacks increased from 14.7 to 24.0 per 1,000. In subsequent years, the death rate for both blacks and whites decreased, but death continued to visit blacks more frequently; data for 1925 and 1930 reveal death rates of 19.4 and 15.6 for blacks, and 10.4 and 8.7 for whites.[56] It is significant that from 1915 to 1941 tuberculosis, a disease associated with unsanitary conditions often found in overcrowded housing,[57] and in the polluted air in the foundries and paint departments in the automotive industry, was the leading cause of death among blacks in Detroit. In 1915 tuberculosis claimed proportionally more than twice as many blacks (207.7 per 1,000) than whites (96.5 per 1,000). The rate of death attributed to tuberculosis continued to rise among blacks, while showing a significant decrease among whites; specifically, in 1920 and 1925 the rate for blacks was 237.0 and 300.2, in contrast to 76.5 and 59.5 per 1,000 for whites. Moreover, as Thomas observed, "There were only four years during this period (1915-1941) when tuberculosis was not the principal cause of death among blacks: 1935, 1939,

1940, and 1941. In those years, heart disease and pneumonia competed with each other in claiming black lives."[58]

Married or single, the housing and working conditions experienced by black workers employed in the Crystal Palace between 1910 and 1927 were worse than the standards or relative comforts achieved by other groups. It is a widely held view that in regard to the employment of black workers, the Ford Motor Company had a more progressive policy than others in the industry; while it is a view supported by much of the evidence, especially the data relevant to employment in the River Rouge plant, it is not a view that is appropriate for the reality of the Crystal Palace. Generally speaking, black workers were found in jobs with the lowest pay scales, jobs that required the greatest physical exertion, had the highest accident rates, and the greatest health hazards. Throughout the industry, it was commonly understood that the most hazardous and least desirable jobs were in and around the foundry, and more often than not, this is where black workers were employed. It was only in the Rouge plant that a significant percentage of blacks were found in some of the more desirable jobs. In fact, in the Rouge plant, blacks were employed in all phases of the manufacturing operation, including final assembly. The situation in the Crystal Palace was entirely different.

According to one researcher, on February 9, 1914, William Perry became the first black employee of the Ford Motor Company. Jim Price, who had apparently come into contact with Charles E. Sorensen, who frequented a tailor shop where Price had been employed, was among the earliest black workers in the Crystal Palace. Price was attracted to the Crystal Palace by the profit-sharing plan and persuaded Sorensen to support his efforts to gain employment in the plant. Price was given a job in the tool crib, and Sorensen said to him, "Jim, you're going to be the first colored man here to get a job that means something."[59]

It should be recalled that the vast majority of the blacks who came to the Detroit area to find work in the automotive industry came in one of two waves. The first wave was part of the "great migration," and came during 1916-1917 to alleviate a labor shortage resulting from the fact that World War I disrupted the flow of immigrants who might normally have been expected to meet labor needs, and the fact that others in the workforce had been drafted or volunteered to do military service. The second wave came during the period 1924-1925 to fill a void in the labor force created by legislation restricting immigration into the United

States. Lewis noted that Ford's policy regarding the employment of blacks was the same as the policy that characterized the Detroit area c.1914-1919. More precisely, noted Lewis, on January 12, 1916, the Ford Motor Company had 32,702 employees, fifty of whom were black.[60] One year later (January 12, 1917) the company counted 36,411 employees and 136 were black; by March the number of blacks employed by Ford had risen only to 200. However, the following year (1918) witnessed an important change in Ford's employment practices.

On the basis of personal contact with Sorensen, the Reverend Robert L. Bradby, pastor of the Second Baptist Church in Detroit, established himself as an "agent" of the Ford Motor Company, and apparently had the authority to issue "passes" allowing selected individuals access to personnel interviewers in the company.[61] Owing, in part, to passes from Bradby, the number of black workers employed by Ford, most notably in the new Rouge plant, increased significantly. In 1918 the company hired 1,059 black men, and in 1919 a total of 1,597 were hired.[62] By 1920, with 1,675 blacks remaining on the payroll, the Ford Motor Company had become the auto industry's leading employer of black workers.[63]

The recession of 1920-1921 and the Great Depression beginning about 1929 and lasting through the early 1930s found many automotive workers out of work, and many never returned to the ranks of those employed in the automotive industry. For those who remained, the Rouge plant was a stronghold of black workers in the Detroit area. Of 8,756 black workers employed by the Ford Motor Company in 1940, all but 200 were employed in the Rouge plant. The Model T assembly line had been shut down in May of 1927, and by 1935 the total number of workers—in what was once the showcase of the automotive industry and the crown jewel of the Ford Motor Company—had been reduced to 2,488 workers, 20 of whom were black. By 1940, only 18 black workers could be found in the Crystal Palace.[64]

By almost every objective standard, the quality housing occupied by the elites of the Crystal Palace—virtually all white-collar employees and many skilled blue-collar workers—was superior to the housing in the densely populated ethnic communities such as those in northeast Detroit. To a large extent, these neighborhoods were occupied by the first cohort of semiskilled and unskilled men who worked on the assembly line and "pooled" much of their family income "in order to buy homes in their tight ethnic communities."[65] In stark contrast to the densely settled

ethnic communities occupied by semiskilled and unskilled workers, Ford's white-collar and skilled workers, who were either
"native" whites or old immigrant stock, did not live in ethnic
neighborhoods but in the new lots near Grand Boulevard or in the
suburban community developed by Henry Ford's real estate company.

P.E. Martin, for example, lived on Trowbridge Street while his
children were small, but moved to a larger home at 1488 Chicago
Boulevard in 1923, and after he became vice president moved to
1411 Wellesly Drive in the prestigious Palmer Woods district.[66] In
1915 Sorensen was transferred from the Highland Park plant to
supervise the Henry Ford & Son Tractor Plant in Dearborn, and at
that time he built a large colonial home on the Rouge River a mile
or so north of Henry Ford's new home in Fair Lane. Howard
Woodward Simpson was hired as chief draftsman of the tractor
plant, and although he did not have power such as that enjoyed
by Martin and Sorensen, he and his wife "immediately moved
into a home on Mason near Park Street in Dearborn, but soon purchased a Ford-built home at 488 Nona Street."[67]

The particulars vary, of course, but the pattern of acquiring
more expensive housing at increasingly greater distances from the
Crystal Palace and nearby ethnic communities is clear. Clarence
Willard Avery began as a "student worker" and Sorensen's assis-
tant in 1912 and quickly became a rising star in the Ford Motor
Company. Before coming to Ford, the Avery family lived at 761
Hurlbut, and in 1911 they moved to 364 Montclair Avenue. While
at Ford the Avery family moved into a new home at 50 Puritan
Avenue in Highland Park. "By 1918 the Averys were at 460 Boston
Boulevard, in an area only recently vacated by Henry Ford himself. Six years later, still working for Ford, Avery purchased a
house at 1560 Wellesly, in exclusive Palmer Woods, very close to
his associate Peter E. Martin."[68]

On a continuum with one end representing the housing conditions found in the ethnic neighborhoods and the other end representing the conditions evident in the exclusive communities
such as Palmer Park, the vast majority of Ford's workers would
be found somewhere near the middle.

Like the physical distances between neighborhoods inhabited
by Ford's white-collar employees and the "ethnic" enclaves, there
was also social and psychological distancing that accompanied
the consolidation of the new social order fostered by the technological and managerial revolutions. According to one interpreta-

tion, the atmosphere or "spirit" of social interaction in the Crystal Palace and the Rouge plant that was mainly created by Martin, Sorensen, Klann, Hartner et al., can be divided into three phases. During the Lee-Marquis-Avery era when the Crystal Palace was called the "House of Good Feeling" (1913-1920), "Highland Park presented in everything but its lack of organization an almost Utopian example of enlightened, kindly, progressive labor relations." The depression of 1920-1921 shook the foundation of the Ford Motor Company and the executives responded with a "speed-up" and "the men found the pace of production accelerated, enforcement of rules tightened, and the whole atmosphere harsher." Thus, the second phase (1920-1923) was defined by a worsening of the "spirit" in the Crystal Palace and the Rouge. In the third phase (1923-1930), as the Model T era approached its end and the Model A and others were ascending, the "spirit" was somewhat restored.[69]

For much of the Model T era the defining quality of the "spirit" of social relations in the Crystal Palace was that the white-collar and skilled workers shared a sense of privilege and behaved as if they were superior beings. As Zunz noted, even though the white-collar employees formed a distinct group, their ranks were regularly broken by blue-collar workers "moving up." Since workers who moved up simply adopted the attitudes of those already in the white-collar class, the collar-line continued to represent a sharp demarcation in the attitudes that separated white- and blue-collar employees. The clearest division, both in the plant and in communities where the employees lived, was one in which not only the clerks kept a distance from workers, but foremen and skilled workers in supervisory positions "also held themselves aloof from semiskilled and unskilled workers." Moreover, the company reinforced and emphasized the separation between foremen and assembly-line workers by placing foremen on the salaried payroll along with office workers.[70]

This attitude is evident in the statement by C.R. Smith, Sr., a record clerk and driver for Sociological Department investigators, who said flatly, that "the foreign born were living like cattle."[71] Foremen such as William C. Klann shared the patronizing attitudes of white-collar management and clerks toward the unskilled workers. "Klann lumped Italians and blacks together in his patronizing assessment: 'A lot of the colored fellows and Italian fellows were the same way. They came from the old country and they had their wives and kids over there.'" Klann's attitude was typical and it is fair to say that "foremen shared the prejudices of white-collar management and the clerks toward unskilled workers."[72]

For much of the first generation of automotive workers, the prevailing "spirit" was like that bitterly recalled by Frederick Winslow Taylor in his later life. "I was a young man in years," Taylor wistfully stated, "but I give you my word I was a great deal older than I am now with the worry, meanness, and comtemptibleness of the whole damn thing. It is a horrid life . . . not to be able to look any workman in the face all day long without seeing hostility."[73] In the Ford Motor Company, the major manifestation, in Taylor's words, of the "horrid life" may be seen in the work of the Sociological Department, and to a lesser extent, in the Americanization program.

6

Ford's Welfare Work: Americanization and the Molding of the Ford Man

It has already been noted that within the historical context of large-scale industrialization during the latter part of the nineteenth century, modern personnel management had its origin in "welfare work" and "scientific management." It has also been noted that "Taylorism" played an important, though indirect, role in the implementation of employment engineering in the Crystal Palace, Ford's main plant in the Detroit area until the opening of the Rouge plant in about 1918. This chapter focuses on the welfare work initiated by Ford's Sociological Department and the Americanization campaign centered in the Ford English School. Both of these initiatives embodied and symbolized the incentive of the famous five-dollar day, and together with the changes in production engineering, complete the triangle of the system of modern personnel management that created the Ford Man.

There is no doubt that the major event in the social and cultural history of Highland Park was the announcement of the profit-sharing plan, better known as the five-dollar day. During meetings early in January 1914, the board of directors of the Ford Motor Company had discussed wages and had allotted $10 million for a profit-sharing plan. In 1916, Samuel Marquis referred to the plan as the "granddaddy of company-initiated reform plans," and explained that the plan involved rationalizing the Ford employment and wage structure by reducing the number of job categories, regularizing pay scales, reducing foremen's power to hire and fire employees, and raising the pay of certain classes of employees to a five-dollar minimum.[1] As simply as this, the basis for the most famous labor-management reform in the annals of American business, the Ford five-dollar day, had been etched into the historical record. As initially conceived, the profit-sharing plan supplemented and extended earlier reforms which, in the rapidly developing tradition of Frederick Winslow Taylor's scientific-management, had been aimed at making the administration of the Ford factory more efficient. In contrast to John R. Lee's reforms of October 1913, emphasizing the more scientific management of labor, the five-dollar day added the extra dimension of welfare activities to the industrial betterment program of the company.[2]

On Monday afternoon of January 5, 1914, the announcement of the reforms came with much fanfare; the press release stated that on January 12, 1914, the Ford Motor Company, "the greatest and most successful [company] in the world would inaugurate the greatest revolution in . . . rewards for workers ever known in the industrial world."[3] The press release explained that the foundation of the revolution was a profit-sharing plan that would increase the minimum daily wage of qualified workers to five dollars; it was also noted that three eight-hour shifts would replace the existing two nine-hour shifts, and that 4,000 more workers would be added to the existing workforce of 15,000. To understand these dramatic developments, and to make an assessment of the overall effectiveness of the Sociological Department in upgrading the quality of life of those working in the Crystal Palace, and to consider how the "Americanization" program contributed to the making of the Ford Worker, it is necessary to understand the context in which the plan was introduced.

In a manner of speaking, Ford profit-sharing was like much of the welfare work common during the early decades of the twentieth century. Rooted, to some extent, in the intellectual traditions of the Social Gospel and Progressivism, "industrial betterment" and "industrial welfare work," as they were then called, were as diverse as the companies in which they were instituted. Among the leaders of the movement to establish industrial welfare work, the National Civic Federation captured the diversity of its policies and programs when it attempted to define the boundaries of industrial betterment. According to the National Civic Federation's definition, industrial betterment or industrial welfare work of the era involved "special consideration for physical comfort wherever labor is performed; opportunities for recreation; educational advantages; the providing of suitable sanitary homes, . . . plans for saving and lending money, and provisions for insurance and pensions."[4] In short, welfare work was aimed at improving the quality of life of industrial workers and their families.

The National Civic Federation definition of welfare work fundamentally conforms to the stated objectives of Ford's profit-sharing plan; and, as far as the definition goes, the Ford Motor Company was like many other companies. But Ford was also different from others in some important ways. For one, Ford was a leading manufacturer and had a tremendous financial capacity, and the zeal and absolute conviction with which the agents in Ford's Sociological Department pursued the Americanization of Ford employees were unparalleled. The evidence of Ford's dedication may be seen in the administration and (to a lesser extent) the results achieved by the Health and Safety program within the Crystal Palace, the efforts of the Sociological Department to upgrade the home and housing conditions among workers, and in the Americanization program.

On the basis of official statements, organizational and operational reforms within the Ford Motor Company, and the reported results of the Sociological Department operations, it is reasonable to conclude that what motivated the Ford Motor Company to develop and implement the profit-sharing plan, of which the five-dollar daily minimum was a part, was the desire to increase profits by increasing efficiency in production, and reducing turnover in the labor force; to give workers a stake in contributing to the increased production, while reshaping the workforce to suit the needs of the new industrial system; and to upgrade the quality of life of the workforce, their families, and their neighborhoods.[5]

Regarding some of the accomplishments attributed to the profit-sharing plan, one top level official remarked that, as evidenced by the fact that with the profit-sharing plan, the "Ford Motor Company made more cars and greater earnings than ever before," and "the Five-Dollar Day was the greatest success for the Ford Motor Company."[6] Another official said, "I think the Ford profit-sharing plan made real citizens out of our employees, out of the type that never had been [real citizens] otherwise."[7] Henry Ford himself had much to say about the profit-sharing plan; he often hastened to assert that the plan was not charity, but profit-sharing based on the level of production and sales; that employees should use their share of the profits to upgrade the quality of their lives; and that the plan was the best cost-cutting device ever introduced by the company. Regarding the reforms associated with the plan, Allan Nevins captured the sentiment most often expressed when he observed, "The enlightened new labor rules, the five-dollar minimum, and the struggle of the Sociological Department to raise living standard constituted, despite inescapable shortcomings, a lustrous chapter in the history of the company and a memorable page in the record of American indus-try."[8]

It has been suggested that part of what motivated the imple-mentation of the profit-sharing plan were diseconomies associ-ated with the enormous turnover in the workforce of the Crystal Palace.[9] Although there were a number of plausible explanations for the high turnover (including the preference for more suitable work elsewhere), John R. Lee's poll of workers during the summer of 1913 revealed that much of the dissatisfaction among workers resulted from work-days that were too long, wages that were too low, unsanitary and otherwise undesirable shop condi-tions, bad housing, and perhaps most important, the unintelligent and often abusive handling of men by foremen and superinten-dents.[10] The combination of factors contributing to dissatisfaction with conditions in the Crystal Palace, and perhaps the availability of work elsewhere, may explain why in December 1912, 776 men were discharged, the highest number in company history; and why in 1913 the Ford Motor Company needed to hire 52,445 men to maintain a workforce of 14,000; and why in March of 1913 the number of "five-day men" (i.e., men quitting without notice or explanation) was 5,156. "Between 50,000 and 60,000 workers passed through Ford's employment office in 1913 when the number of employees was only 13,600; the company needed to hire between 40% and 60% of its labor force every month to main-tain it."[11] In any case, the high turnover was undoubtedly a com-pelling argument for the worker reform package introduced the following year.[12]

The reforms, sometimes referred to as the "Lee Reforms," to which the profit-sharing plan was a supplement, were imple-mented in 1913. Apparently in response to the worker dissatisfac-tion recorded in the poll taken during the summer,[13] on Octo-ber 12, 1913, the Ford Motor Company introduced a 15% wage increase, implemented a new skill-wages classification system, and created the Employee's Savings and Loan Association. The skill-wage classification system was based on an analysis of the content of each job, and the subsequent classification and ranking of each job according to skill-level. "The new system," Lee con-cluded, "was a broad plan for the stratification of workers in the plant along clearly defined lines and on the basis of definite stan-dards."[14] In addition to the new system of classifying jobs, and the creation of the Employee's Savings and Loan Association, the Ford Employment Office was reorganized and became the Ford

Employment Department. The latter was a major change that gradually resulted in the centralization of the functions previously in the foreman's domain; ultimately, the department became responsible for all phases of labor relations.

Having allotted $10 million to the profit-sharing plan, the board of directors appointed John R. Lee to implement the plan, and left it to him to work out the details. Among Lee's first actions was the establishment of the department that would shoulder the primary responsibility for implementing the plan. Reflecting the apparent fact that sociology had "matured and gained acceptance as an academic discipline for the study, analysis, and management of the affairs of men," the Sociological Department was named after a similar institution in Rockefeller's Colorado Fuel and Iron Company. In 1914, O.J. Abell estimated that the Sociological Department was staffed by about 100 investigators, including physicians on the medical staff, and others who were among the trusted employees of the Ford Motor Company; again, according to Abell, later in 1914 the Sociological Department numbered about 200, before leveling off to a permanent staff of 50 persons.[15] On July 3, 1915, an internal source reported, contrary to Abell's estimates, that the Sociological Department then consisted of about 20 men who were all that remained of the initial appointment of 75.[16] Here, the accuracy of Abell's estimates is not at issue. The disparity between the estimates of Abell, an astute outsider with privileged access, and those of internal sources may suggest that the Sociological Department appeared to be larger than it was in actuality, and was doing more than could be sustained by its resources. In any case, whatever the number on the staff, it set out to accomplish tasks of enormous proportions and scope that were unprecedented in the annals of welfare capitalism.[17]

From the outset, the central task of the Sociological Department was to determine whether or not workers were eligible to participate in the profit-sharing plan, and to advise those who were not immediately eligible how the might become qualified to share in the profits of the company. In order to determine eligibility, the Sociological Department investigated everyone employed, except high level managers and supervisors. Those investigated included salesmen, foremen, clerks, and factory workers. In one particular instance, when John Lee sent Jack Smith to investigate his brother-in-law William C. Klann, who was Clarence Avery's assistant and a top-level foreman, "Klann simply refused to let his relative proceed with the investigation." "As Klann put it, we were trying to teach other fellows how to live and they wanted to investigate us at the same time." The matter was settled by putting Klann on the Sociological Department honor roll, together with Ed Harper, Charlie Hartner, Avery, Perini, and other foremen, where they helped the department investigate other men."[18]

The determination of eligibility was largely at the discretion of the investigators, all of whom were apparently "good Ford men" of the type the company hoped to create. It was not until early 1915 that the Sociological Department's "Instructions for Investigators" emerged with detailed methods for the determination of eligibility. In essence, the instructions codified the criteria that had been used up to that point: generally speaking, in order to qualify a worker had to exhibit or demonstrate thrift, good habits, and good home conditions.[19] Additionally, in an effort to stem the flood of job seekers who appeared at the gates of the Crystal Palace shortly after the announcement of the five-dollar day, a six-month residency in the Detroit area became a condition of eligibility.

With thriftiness, good habits, good home conditions, and six-month residency as the basis for qualifying, 10% of the employees failed to qualify on the basis of age or sex (unmarried men and females were categorically excluded from profit-sharing), and another 40% could not qualify without changing their lives in order to meet the conditions prescribed by Ford.[20] Not only was there an age and sex bias against participation in the plan, but the fact that 1,381 of the first 14,000 employees to qualify were of British ancestry also strongly suggests that there was a bias against the "ethnics."[21] To a large extent then, the mission of the Sociological Department was to reform the ethnics so that they might qualify for participation in the plan, and in the process a supply of workers who ideally suited the needs of production in the Crystal Palace would be molded.

The manner in which the work of the Sociological Department initially organized and distributed its assignments may be seen in a variety of official reports and the "reminiscences" of the Sociological Department staff and other officials of the company, as well as in statements made by some of the ethnics who were the intended objects of reform. Together, these sources demonstrate that it was believed that the desired reform depended on the creation, or the restoration and maintenance, of "good home conditions." In short, as Stephen Meyer has put it, "A fundamental premise of the Ford program was a particular middle-class vision of the role of the family and the home in the formation of social and cultural values."[22] S.S Marquis expressed the sentiment that appears to have dominated official thinking in the Ford Motor Company about the relationship of cultural values to production in the Crystal Palace when he stated that "the family is the foundation of the church and the state." Moreover, continued Marquis, "We found that it is the foundation of right industrial conditions as well. Nothing tends to lower a man's efficiency more than wrong family relations."[23]

Chapter 7 of this study discusses the home and housing conditions of Ford workers in Highland Park more fully, but for the moment it should be noted that most observers believed that there was indeed room for improvement, and that as a factor which promised to increase efficiency in production, there can be no doubt that the Ford Motor Company took seriously the goal of uplifting and improving its workers. From another perspective, it is apparent that the commitment to improve production through improving home and housing conditions was part of a general effort aimed at "Americanizing" the workforce employed in the Crystal Palace.

According to an extensive survey conducted under the auspices of the Committee on Public Information in 1918 (February to June), "Americanizing" the industrial workforce was a multidimensional movement that included private and voluntary, state and municipal, and federal involvement.[24] Three overlapping but distinct phases and two groups of protagonists may be seen in the Americanization movement. The first phase was clearly in evidence when, by the end of the century, a movement to encourage the "Americanization" of the new immigrants had begun to stir.[25] A second phase evolved out of "the wartime drive for unity, spearheaded by Creel's Committee on Public Information, led naturally to a campaign for accelerated "Americanization" of newcomers.[26] A third phase is marked by a postwar economy that saw both prosperity and depression, and an intensified, more militant effort to organize the workforce. This phase also witnessed government involvement to a degree that had not been anticipated by management. Throughout these three phases, proponents of the Americanization movement expressed views, supported objectives, and implemented programs often in conflict with each other.

David M. Kennedy and John Higham have suggested one element that may be associated with the first phase of the Ameri-

canization movement consisted of settlement-house workers and
social reformers, among whom Lillian Wald, Jane Addams, and
Josephine Roche, and many people associated with the American
Union Against Militarism were prominent. In this faction, the first
concern was for the immigrants themselves; they strove to mini-
mize the stresses of assimilation by providing a receptive environment for Old World cultures. The countervailing faction in the
Americanization movement was a coalition that consisted of "old-
stock Americans who feared for the continued ascendancy of their
cultural values and social position, and businessmen who sought
to discipline a troublesomely varied labor force."[27] But the war
cemented the loose coalition of business interests and, if only tem-
porarily, drove the reformist (Progressive) faction into the camp
harboring business interests.

Generally speaking, industrialists did not concern themselves
with Americanization until the labor shortages of 1914 presented
the specter of production levels far below demand. Notable
exceptions before 1910 include International Harvester, which
wanted workers to become "good Americans" while learning to
think and talk intelligently about important operations in the factory.[28] As early as 1907, the industrial secretary of the YMCA,
Peter Roberts, had started a language and citizenship program for
factory workers, and he ably adjusted the program to the needs of
corporations.[29]

In the Detroit area, the Ford Motor Company led manufacturers in adopting Americanization objectives. The seed of what
would become a full-blown Americanization campaign in 1914
could be found in the *Ford Times* in 1908 when it incessantly
exhorted Ford workers (primarily Americans and Germans at this
time) to ingest the American work ethic. One example of many
early entreaties was embodied in a New Year's resolution for Ford
workers that stated, "Of my own free will and accord, I sincerely
covenant with myself, . . . To exalt the Gospel of Work, . . . To
Keep head, heart, and hand so busy that I won't have time to
think of my troubles. Because idleness is a disgrace, low aim is
criminal, and work minus its spiritual quality becomes
drudgery."[30] While the Ford Motor Company would take the lead
during the second phase in Americanizing workers in the Detroit
area (actually, throughout the United States), the "Americanization movement at Ford was not an isolated eccentric phenomenon, but a well publicized symptom of a general trend in
Detroit";[31] and Ford's program was recognized as "One of the

most extensive and best organized efforts made by an industry for the Americanization of foreign-born."[32] Its success was so impressive to "local proponents of Americanization activities that they convinced the Detroit Board of Commerce to promote Ford's methods in other local factories." Thus, what had started as a purely economic program at the Ford plant soon became the basis of a broad patriotic and nationalistic endeavor.[33]

In an effort to replicate and disseminate the program operating in the Crystal Palace and Highland Park, in 1915 the Detroit Board of Commerce created the Detroit Americanization Committee, whose primary official purpose included the promotion and inculcation of the principles of American institutions and good citizenship, and the exhortation and assistance of immigrants "to learn the English language, the history, laws and government of the United States, the rights and duties of citizenship; and in becoming intelligent Americans."[34] In the same year the National Americanization Committee, under the leadership of Frances Kellor, was formed with the more limited goal of celebrating national Independence Day by bringing together "all Americans, wherever born."[35]

From its inception, the Detroit Americanization movement was dominated by the large employers of the city, and "they set the tone and policy."[36] The eleven-member Americanization Committee of Detroit, actually a subcommittee of the Detroit Board of Commerce, included six representatives of Detroit's leading corporations: Henry W. Hoyt, vice president of the Great Lakes Engineering Company; F.S. Bigler, president of Michigan Bolt and Nut Company; Ernest L. Lloyd, president of Lloyd Construction Company; John R. Lee, director of the Ford Sociological Department; Horace Rackham, an attorney and capitalist who was Henry Ford's legal counsel; and W.E. Scripps of the Scripps Motor Company, Scripps-Booth Cycle Car Company, and the *Detroit News*. In addition to those representing business and industry, the committee included Frank D. Cody, assistant superintendent of the city schools, A.J. Tuttle, United States District Court Judge, A.G. Studer, general secretary of the Y.M.C.A., and Oscar B. Marx, who was mayor of the city and a businessman.[37] David Allan Levine noted that the committee included two other members who deserved mention. One was Fred Butsel, a Jewish attorney who was always interested in social causes and who would appear among the leadership of the Detroit Urban League. The second was Chester M. Culver, who like Butsel would also appear in the affairs of the Detroit Urban League. Culver was general manager of the Employer's Association of Detroit (EAD), unquestionably the most powerful group in the city, and every worker, whatever his nationality or race, was in some way dependent upon it. Often, he was dependent in ways he would never know.[38]

As stated by one Ford official in 1914, "It is our aim and object to make better men and better American citizens, and to bring about a larger degree of comforts, habits, and higher plane of living among our employees. . . ."[39] Meyer has pointed out that in some ways Ford's Americanization program was unique, and in other ways it was like the Americanization programs of other manufacturers and industrialists. Although there were many Americanization programs, and perhaps because of the vigor with which Ford's efforts were publicized, the Ford program served as a model for the National Americanization Day Committee and its national campaign for the assimilation of immigrants into American society.[40] If the profit-sharing plan was the principal instrument through which Ford's workers would become Americanized, and the work to upgrade home and housing conditions was a major component of Americanization, then the Ford English (language) School was the avenue where full assimilation could be ensured.

The organizer of the Ford English School, which coincidentally was first located in the old Stevens School, was Peter Roberts, who was hired by the Ford Motor Company in April 1914. Roberts, an educator who was officially associated with the Y.M.C.A., had published an English language textbook (*English for Coming Americans*, 1909), which became the foundation for the instruction of immigrant workers of the Crystal Palace. "The core of the program centered around domestic, commercial, and an industrial series of lessons which applied the English language to different aspects of the immigrant worker's life."[41] As described by Marquis in 1916, the Ford English School, established for immigrants employed in the Crystal Palace, provided five compulsory courses: "There is a course in industry and efficiency, a course in thrift and economy, a course in domestic relations, one in community relations, and one in industrial relations."[42]

A 1916 report on the Ford English School revealed that in a class of 518 workers, there were 163 Poles, 134 Russians, 46 Austrians, 28 Italians, 23 Hungarians, 20 Germans, 16 Rumanians, 13 Jews, and 11 Bohemians. The remainder of the 518 persons enrolled, presumably fewer than 10 in any one group, represented 28 nationalities.[43] Apparently owing, at least in part, to the efforts of the language school and the incentive of profit-sharing, between 1914 and 1917 the percentage of English speaking employees rose from 59% to 88% (see Table 6.1).[44] From 1915 to 1916, the company reported that some 16,000 workers graduated from the Ford English School, and Ford statistics indicate that while 35.5% of the workforce did not speak English in 1914, only 11.7% did not speak English in 1917.[45]

While speaking the English language may have been the most readily observable sign of the transformation of immigrant workers, Ford officials believed that marital status, home owner- ship, a savings account, and life insurance were important indica- tors of a worker's desire and willingness to be transformed into the preferred type of worker. Table 6.1 suggests that there was a steady increase in the percentage of workers in the Crystal Palace who succeeded in fitting into the mold of the preferred type of worker. The ability of a greater percentage of Ford workers to speak the English language and improvements in home and hous- ing conditions may be considered as indications of the Ford Motor Company's commitment to improving the quality of life of Ford's workers, while improving efficiency in production. Further evidence of Ford's overall commitment to upgrading the quality of life among Ford workers may be seen in the health and safety in the Crystal Palace.

Consistent with the objective of upgrading the quality of life of Ford workers, the Ford Motor Company was apparently very much concerned with safety, even though many production work- ers vehemently disputed that such a concern was paramount in the Crystal Palace. A superior safety record during much of the 1910s and 1920s resulted in the Ford Motor Company's being ranked at the top of the list that rated the results of health and safety programs of automobile manufacturers; many considered this ranking as evidence of Ford's efforts and concerns with regard to safety. The Health and Safety Department was created as part of the 1914 reforms, and in addition to providing a variety of medical services, the newly instituted department issued monthly accident reports and published lists including a variety of physical conditions and diseases that existed among employees. Table 6.2 is based on data recorded by the Health and Safety Department; it suggests that despite concerted efforts and a superior safety record, both occupational diseases and injuries resulting from

Table 6.1
Some Characteristics of Ford's Crystal Palace Employees:
A Comparison by Percent for 1914-1916

Characteristic	1914	1915	1916
Married	59	76	70
Citizens	39	45	51
English Speaking	64	76	87
Buying or Owning:			
a home	12	27	27
a lot	6	11	14
With Bank Accounts	44	66	42
With Life Insurance	19	43	48

Ford Motor Company Archive, Accession 62, Box 59/ Note: A complete set of data is not available for 1917. However, it is known that in 1917 24,533 workers in the Crystal Palace were married, and 9,335 were single. See Ford Motor Company Archive, Accession 572, Box 27.

accidents contributed significantly to the poor physical condition of many of those employed in the Crystal Palace.

In the automotive industry, as well as elsewhere in the industrial world, there were and still are occupational hazards that may have deleterious effects on the health of workers. Occupational hazards include accidental injury and conditions in the workplace environment that may be considered to be "normal" but are associated with the cause of certain diseases. In 1916 Horace Arnold and Fay Faroute reported on the notoriously unhealthy conditions in the foundry. It was noted that foundry workers suffered from severe heat and lack of ventilation, and "the air during the work hours cannot be endured by workmen save those possessing respiratory organs of the most robust description, and many visitors are unable to walk through the Ford greyiron foundry . . . because they cannot breathe the air."[46] Conditions such as those described by Arnold and Faroute and conditions in other parts of the factory have been associated with particular abnormalities. Lowery observed that jobs connected with painting and metal finishing carried the most severe health problems in the auto industry; lead poisoning, tuberculosis and silicosis led the list of job related diseases.[47] Clearly, among other abnormalities, Table 6.2 shows that in 1925, 629 workers in the Crystal Palace were experiencing serious respiratory problems.

Table 6.2 also records that amputated limbs were a major source of incapacity among employees in the Crystal Palace. Specifically, there were 1,390 amputated fingers, 121 legs, 13 hands, and 31 amputated feet. It comes as no surprise, then, that in the Ford Motor Company the most common cause of permanent disability in the early 1920s was the loss of fingers or parts of fingers.[48] It has been widely publicized that the Ford Motor Company made a concerted effort to hire disabled workers who might be found in the Detroit area. One official recalled that in the 1920s it was no longer necessary to look outside the Ford "family" to find handicapped workers, "we had enough of our own company liabilities to take care of. . . . It helped the employee and the Ford Motor Company. The company didn't have to pay workmen's comp because the man was employed."[49] Despite the high number of injuries, it is quite clear that most injuries were "slight."

The Michigan Department of Labor classified injuries resulting from accidents as fatal, serious, severe, or slight. A survey of reports published during the period under consideration shows that in the Crystal Palace the vast majority of injuries were slight. While there is a wide variation in the number of days that slightly injured persons were disabled (0-24), it was not possible, except in cases of the more extreme severe injuries, to determine by the number of days lost whether the injury was slight or severe.[50] While injuries of all classes appear evenly distributed among the various age groups of employees, a sample of injuries reported during 1914 reveals that there was a disproportionately large number of injuries in the 18-25 age group at a time when the mode was 25 and the median age was about 30 years of age.[51]

With what has been shown about occupational hazards, it may be argued that in 1914 the high rate of injury among employees 18-25 years of age is associated with a greater exposure to high-risk jobs, inexperience on the part of workers, and perhaps, to production line "speed-ups," etc. It can also be argued that in contrast to the mode of 25 years of age in 1916, the mode in 1914 was lower, and this characteristically lower age in 1914 is the best

Table 6.2
Physically Substandard Employees in the Crystal Palace
Tabulated from Information on 44,500 Workers

Condition		Number
Chest: TBC, serious lung trouble, asthma		629
Deaf, and deaf and dumb		111
Epileptics and mental conditions		187
Eyes: Blind		51
Blind in one eye		187
Bad Vision	1,032	
Feet: Amputated		31
Toes amputated		104
Deformed, crippled, etc.		312
Hands: Fingers amputated		1,390
Hands amputated		13
Deformed, crippled, etc.		227
Heart: High blood pressure		417
Hernias (conservative estimate)		5,000
Kidneys and bladder (conservative estimate)		800
Legs: Amputated		121
Deformed, crippled, etc.		423
Nervousness		122
Paralysis		56
Rheumatism/arthritis		505
Spine and Back		264
Stomach (ulcers)		552
Miscellaneous: anemia, bladder, cancer, deformed, cripples, dropsy, gall stones, goiter, head fractures, hemorrhoids, locomotor staxa, sleeping sickness, and temporary concessions for bronchitis, gastritis, nose, throat and head conditions, etc.		650

Source: Ford Motor Company Archive, Accession 940, Box 16, "Samuel
M. Levin Papers" dated April 25, 1925.

Table 6.3
A Sample of Injuries in the Crystal Palace
Recorded During 1914-1915

Years of Age	Number of Injuries	
	1914	1915
18-25	100	78
25-30	54	93
30-35	7	48
35-40	25	30
40-45	13	22
45-50	8	15
50-55	4	7
55-60	2	1
60-65	-	1
65-75	-	-
75-85	-	-
TOTAL	236	295

Source: "Record of Accidents Given by Counties," in Michigan Department of Labor *Thirty-first Annual Report* 1914, 315-21; and Michigan Department of Labor *Thirty-second Annual Report* 1915, 367-72. Note: Injuries to workers under 21 years of age: 1914 (390 in sample) 22; 1915 (300 in sample) 10.

explanation of the comparatively high number of injuries to employees 18-25 in 1914. The sample of 295 injuries reported in 1915 reveals a more even distribution among the workers whose age closely approximated the median. (See Appendix A, Table A.5.)

Accidental injuries involving Ford workers under age 21 need to be analyzed within the context of their employment in metal-manufacturing in Michigan. The Children's Bureau of the U.S. Department of Labor conducted a study of representative metal-manufacturing companies in Michigan. This study reported that 11% of all employees were persons under 21 years of age; of those under 21 years of age, 99% were over 16, and about two-thirds were between 19 and 21.[52] In 1918, "there were 1,905 industrial accidents to minors resulting in death, dismemberment, or incapacity for work lasting from 15 days to 1 year. A large number of these accidents occurred in the metal-working industries,"[53] in which the auto industry was a major employer. The record of accidental injuries in the Crystal Palace and elsewhere in the Ford Motor Company must be seen within this larger context.

During 1914 there were about 390 recorded injuries in the Crystal Palace, 22 involving workers who were 21 or fewer years of age. All of the reported injuries in this age group were classified as "slight." F. Syzmerski, age 16, was injured on March 11, 1914, and was disabled for one day; and W. Johnson, also age 16, was injured on October 13 and disabled for four days. Syzmerski and Johnson were the youngest among workers who reported injuries. All other injured workers were 18 or more years of age, and most of these were 19 or 20 years of age. The year 1915 recorded a dramatic decrease in injuries to workers under 21 years of age; a total of about 300 injuries among all workers were reported, and 10 of these involved this youthful group. Again, there are several plausible explanations for the significant decrease in injuries to workers of this age group. The decrease most probably resulted from a combination of the decrease in the number of young workers employed in production, and the comparatively vigorous safety program of Ford's Health and Safety Department. Assuming that improvements were not simply the result of better record keeping, the Ford Motor Company is deserving of praise for what appears as improvement in its own safety record among its youngest employees, while establishing itself as a leader among firms involved in metal-manufacturing. However, as shown in Table 6.3, the record of injuries to workers between the ages of 25 and 40 is considerably less deserving of commendation.

In sum, the Ford Motor Company's apparent commitment to improving the quality of life among its workers by upgrading home and housing conditions, by Americanizing the workforce, and by minimizing the risk of injury in the Crystal Palace and other facilities had a dual motive. Martha Banta aptly captured the essence of Ford's efforts in noting that "Taylorism and its progeny quickly became synonymous for systems of control," and during the Avery-Lee-Marquis years (1914-21) the Ford idea was "to increase man's capacity for happiness and at the same time increase his efficiency, his earning capacity, and his worth in society, so that he may have access to the things he has been taught to enjoy."[54]

In other words, Ford's efforts were based on the assumption that an improved quality of life was essential to the achievement of optimal efficiency in production. Despite the duality in motivation, several objective indicators of the quality of life suggest that during the era of the Sociological Department, the quality of life experienced by the labor force producing the Model T was higher (i.e., set the standard) than that of other automotive workers in the Detroit area. The comparatively high quality of life of the builders of the Model T was achieved at the expense of a loss of privacy, autonomy, and perhaps, dignity and self-esteem. Ford officials and journalistic writers and many of the workers have often disagreed on whether the end justified the means. One critic's remarks seem to summarize the thinking most often encountered by this researcher. Ida Tarbell, the famous muckraker who visited the Crystal Palace with the intention of exposing the abuses of Ford's paternalism, was so thoroughly impressed by what she saw that she told the Detroit Executive Club, "I don't care what you call it—philanthropy, paternalism, autocracy—the results which are being obtained are worth all you can set against them, and the errors in the plan will provoke their own remedies."[55]

7

Ford-Men Living In:
Boarding and Boarders in Highland Park
and Vicinity, 1910-1927

Since the vast majority of boarders were unmarried men or married men separated from their families, and since Ford's Sociological Department was encouraging the establishment of "normal American households" as part of an effort to create the ideal worker, it was widely believed among Ford officials that a major obstacle to the creation and maintenance of the "desired" home condition was the presence of boarders. Given that boarders created an undesirable home environment, and an undesirable home environment was believed to affect the productive capacities of Ford workers, it followed that the presence of boarders in the households of Ford workers was believed to have reduced production in the Crystal Palace. According to Ida Tarball, who interviewed Henry Ford extensively in 1915, "Mr Ford knew that, do all for a man in the factory—a short day, higher wages, good conditions, training, advancement—if things are not right for him at home he will not in the long run be a good workman." And Ford believed that with boarders present "things could not be right at home." "So he set out the reorganize the home life of the men."[1] S.S. Marquis summed up the sentiment that appears to have dominated the Ford Motor Company's official thinking about boarders, stating that "the family is the foundation of the church and the state. We found that it is the foundation of right industrial conditions as well. Nothing tends to lower a man's efficiency more than wrong family relations."[2]

During the seventeenth, eighteenth, and much of the nineteenth century, boarding was one of the major ways in which the biologically defined limits of the American family were commonly breached "by an instrumental relationship based on economic and service exchange."[3] John Modell and Tamara K. Hareven have outlined what appears to be a universally appropriate assessment of the motives and immediate consequences of taking in boarders. While characteristics of the housing market, variances in income, employment, and demographic changes all affected the overall pattern of boarding, it is evident that economic factors were primary considerations. Families that took in boarders profited in a variety of ways: 1) they were able to receive a "brokerage fee" for adapting dwelling places of various sizes to the needs of (usually) unmarried immigrants of their own social level and standard of living; 2) they earned an income for work performed by the wife or other woman who was recognized as the authoritative female in the household; 3) they acquired possible access to an income during periods of illness or unemployment; and 4) they made it possible for many widows and single women in their forties, fifties, and sixties to maintain their own households rather than live with their relatives.[4] Clearly, the practice of taking in boarders had its advantages.

In the shadows of the Crystal Palace—Highland Park and neighboring communities—the boarding of Ford workers was big business; in fact some houses, like those on Manchester near the McGregor Library, were built with the idea of boarding in mind.[5] The "want ads" sections of area newspapers carried the call of those seeking board and those seeking boarders. A typical advertisement read, "Wanted 2 men in good German home, near Ford factory: steam heat, privileges, good meals $8 Hem 2584-R." Similarly, another ad read, "Protestant Christian Ford Man can partly pay for room and board by occasional driving of lady's car: References. Near Palmer Park, Box 18, HP."[6] While advertisements may suggest that boarding was a big business, there is no doubt that most boarders found their way to rooming houses through word of mouth, and they most likely roomed in households where the ethnic, economic, and social realities were similar to their own.

Despite the apparent social, psychological and economic benefits of taking in boarders, by 1910 the widespread practice of "boarding and lodging within the family had been under attack for a quarter century."[7] With the large influx of immigrants beginning in the 1870s, the practice of boarding and lodging had come under attack from certain reform-minded persons, and by the end of the nineteenth century the noted housing reformer Lawrence Veiller and other Progressive reformers had begun to refer to the institution of boarding and lodging as "the lodger evil."[8] Veiller wrote that "room overcrowding as we know it in America is almost entirely wrapped up with the lodger evil." He continued, "Aside from its impact on the family, lodging and boarding was clearly associated with the decline of neighborhoods and with social disorder."[9] Some conditions described by Modell and Hareven could be found in Highland Park, and by 1914 Ford officials were also concerned about the negative consequences of boarding.

Housing conditions in sections of Highland Park were abominable. According to the description of a local newspaper, Ford workers had "taken up living quarters in thoroughfares that formerly were delightful, exclusive residence streets, crowding the dwellings to their utmost capacity." Apparently, "there were a number of houses in Highland Park in which these foreigners used the beds in three shifts of eight hours each 24 hours a day. These houses had beds in practically every room, even renting out cots in the attic and bath rooms."[10] Home and housing conditions were such that in 1917 Henry Ford himself "toyed with the idea of building an extensive housing complex divided into areas to house different ethnic groups, each with its own community center, school and stores."[11] As early as 1914, Ford officials had been expressing a dim view of the consequences of boarding on the quality of life of Ford workers, and its impact on production in the Crystal Palace.

That the Ford Motor Company took the presence of boarders seriously may be seen in a variety of records and reports kept by the Sociological Department. In 1916 Boris Emmet published the story of a worker whose living conditions were believed to be typical of the new immigrants.[12] This particular worker was a German Catholic who had migrated from the German area of Poland, and whose family consisted of a wife and four children in 1914. The Sociological Department investigator described the worker as having "poor habits," which included drinking and smoking. The investigator described the worker's environment as a neighborhood of foreigners living in one- and two-story frame houses all apparently in poor condition. Of course, the investigator noted that the neighborhood was unacceptable for the habitation of a Ford man. "This man," wrote the investigator, "lives in a dirty unsanitary hut and has a room full of boarders, who sleep 3 and 4 to a room. Some of the boarders go through the room where the man and his wife sleep to reach their room." Moreover, the investigator added, "The wife looks haggard from overwork. She and the children are as dirty as their surroundings.[13]

Similarly undesirable conditions were reported by other investigators. William Pickel found one worker, his wife and three children, along with four male roomers, living in one room that was partitioned by a cheap curtain.[14] Another investigator reported the situation of a worker named Joe Kostruba, who, along with his wife and children, had emigrated (c.1912) from Russia. Kostruba reportedly lived in Highland Park at 812 Beaubien Street. The house was described as a one-and-a-half-story frame house which was old and tumbledown. At the time of the investigation, the house was occupied by the Kostruba family, consisting of a wife and six children ranging in age from 12 years to a nursing baby, and three other families, one of which was a black family.[15]

In cases such as those described, which were apparently quite common among workers in the Crystal Palace, the investigators would normally refuse to certify the worker as eligible to participate in the profit-sharing plan; or the investigator might find that the worker was eligible to participate, but only on the condition that the additional income provided by participation be used to maintain home conditions comparable to those exhibited by the Armenian machine operator whose story was reported by Harry F. Porter. According to Porter, the Sociological Department investigator stated that this Armenian worker was a Catholic who had been living in the Detroit area for three to five years. The worker boarded in an apartment consisting of five rooms and a bath, and occupied by two men and one woman.[16]

Another interesting case of a "reformed" worker was recorded by Emmet. Having been advised by the investigator to discontinue the practice of taking in boarders and to move to a better neighborhood, a German Catholic worker, who had been found living in a "dirty unsanitary hut," but apparently in a fashion typical of workers who were initially denied participation in the profit-sharing plan, "purchased a lot in the suburbs on which was built a three room structure where he and his family lived without boarders." By August 1915, the investigator rewarded the reformed worker by approving him for participation in the plan, and in December the investigator reported, "Our employee is making wonderful progress with his share of the profits. His home is comfortably furnished; the family is neat and clean." Furthermore, the investigator added, "He can now speak English, and he has taken out first naturalization papers."[17] It appears that the incentive of profit-sharing was so great, and the guidance of the Sociological Department investigators so persuasive, that 13,000 families moved during the first year of the plan.

It is impossible to know from existing evidence how much living standards may have changed and the precise impact the Sociological Department may have had in improving the percentage of "good home conditions." Table 7.1 suggests that some changes probably occurred in home conditions, quality of neighborhoods, and the habits of those who worked in the Crystal Palace. Specifically, Table 7.1 shows changes in the ratio of "poor home conditions" to "good home conditions": 23% "poor" to 47% "good" in 1914; 3% to 70% in 1915; and 2% to 87% in 1916. By 1917 88% of the workers' homes were rated "good," 10% "fair" and 2% "poor." Not surprisingly, Canadian and English workers had the highest percentage of "good" homes, 97% and 96%, respectively; while 75% of the Italian, and 76% of the Rumanian homes were rated "good."[18]

For many workers in 1914, especially the ethnics, the prospects of establishing what the Ford Motor Company considered "good home conditions" were not good, and by 1920 the prospects had diminished considerably. According to Marquis, a "genuine" housing shortage existed, and therefore Ford softened its preference for single-family dwellings. Marquis stated, "In the old days, if a worker lived in bad housing we could tell him to get it straightened out, now we beg the Board of Health to let him stay in a condemned house."[19] Whatever the motives and the net effect of the Sociological Department's efforts to improve the home and housing conditions of Ford workers, the record shows many cases where the Sociological Department was directly responsible for improved conditions.

One case is especially interesting, not only because of the exceptionally large number of boarders involved, but because it also attests to the importance of the income earned by taking in boarders. In this case, a married workman lived in a rented house with his wife and five children. In addition to the worker's family there were eighteen boarders living in the house. "The investigator found that the couple, neither of whom spoke English, . . . had rented [the] house for $80 a month and were realizing a gross income of more than $300 monthly. This and the husband's factory earnings had enabled them to save $890."[20] The workman, of course, was not approved for participation in the profit-sharing plan. This case apparently warranted special attention, and after effort on the part of the investigators, the workman was

Table 7.1
Comparative Status of Living Conditions
of Crystal Palace Workers, As Determinied
by Sociological Department Investigations,
1914, 1915 and 1916 by Percent

		Year	
Status	1914	1915	1916
Home Condition:			
Good	47	70	87
Fair	30	28	11
Poor	23	3	2
Neighborhood:			
Good	41	66	81
Fair	40	32	18
Poor	19	2	1
Habits:			
Good	80	66	73
Fair	19	33	26
Poor	1	1	1
Citizenship:	39	45	51

Source: FMCA Accession 62, Box 59/ "Social Statistics of Home Plant as of January 12, 1916."

persuaded to invest part of his savings in a house on the outskirts of the city. After three months he was put on the profit-sharing plan, and the investigator found that the family had been transformed.

Many observers, especially those close to the Ford Motor Company, applauded the contributions that the profit-sharing plan made to the improvement in the quality of life of some Ford workers and their families. For example, one investigator wrote, "It is more than one year that I have been working in the Sociological Department of the Ford Motor Company, and I am glad to substantiate that our investigative work has been highly successful and that a significant progress is evident regarding the home and living conditions of our employees and their understanding of the intentions of the profit-sharing plan."[21]

However, it is quite possible that, like many assessments recorded by Sociological Department investigators, the statement by John Clarken, who was the Chief Housing Inspector of the Board of Health of the City of Detroit, may be biased in its confirmation that housing conditions of Ford's employees did improve. Clarken wrote that "it has been my observation that the conditions under which the Ford employees are living have been greatly improved, especially in certain sections of the city where they live in large numbers."[22] Despite biases in reports regarding the improved conditions of Ford workers, there is no doubt that, owing to the work of the Sociological Department, and Ford's real estate and housing construction companies, the conditions did improve for some workers. Nevertheless, there is also considerable evidence suggesting that the improvement was not constant and that not all Ford workers benefited equally.

Speaking in favor of a cooperative housing plan on June 25, 1920, Edsel B. Ford remarked, "There seems to be an impression that housing conditions are improving. This idea is not borne out by actual conditions. Housing conditions in this area are just not so acute because large numbers are for the summer living in tents and shacks which will not furnish them proper shelter in the winter." Ford also noted that reports from the public schools showed that large numbers of families were leaving the city, and it appeared therefore that conditions had improved. More important, added Ford, "The houses for sale and rent in the city at the present time are still beyond the reach of the man earning from $6.00-$7.00 per day. This class of men makes up the bulk of our employees."[23]

It appears, then, that the home and housing conditions of many Ford workers improved during the early phase of the profit-sharing plan; that conditions of many other workers were not at all affected; and that the conditions experienced by other workers certainly deteriorated during the early 1920s. Moreover, as suggested by Edsel Ford's statement, a given worker's home conditions were likely to have changed with the seasons and the production schedule; perhaps, changing from "fair" to "good," to "poor" in a continuing cycle of "feast and famine." Whatever the overall state of home and housing conditions of Ford workers, the program to upgrade those conditions was but part of a larger effort aimed at "Americanizing" the workforce, and thereby (it was believed) improving productivity.

One way to get a sense of what life was like in communities in the vicinity of the Crystal Palace, and how it differed from one block to the next, is to develop a profile based on samples from the various neighborhoods of the area. For the purpose of developing such a profile (composite, snapshot or panorama), samples of two distinctly different types of neighborhoods found in Highland Park have been selected for analysis. The first type of neighborhood may be described as having a decidedly greater proportion (more than 90%) of households with "families" consisting of a married couple and one or more of their children and/or some other blood-related relatives. The second type of neighborhood is one in which the vast majority of households included three or more boarders who were not (apparently) blood-related to the head of the household, or to the spouse. More specifically, the neighborhoods selected for consideration are districts number 3 and 7 as demarcated in the 1915 Highland Park special census; an exemplary household on Highland Avenue in square 3, and a few representative households on Labelle and Pasadena streets in square 7 have been singled out for analysis.

When the Ford Motor Company began to manufacture the Model T in the Highland Park plant in 1910, only a very small percentage of those whose lives would later revolve around the production of the Model T had arrived in the Detroit area. This small group of employees was numerically insignificant, but in certain aspects of their lives, they set the standards Ford would attempt to recreate in those who would soon arrive in Highland Park. Among those who are known to have been living in the area before the construction of the Crystal Palace, Pioch, Brown and Siess are probably representative of early Ford employees who had settled in the Highland Park area before 1910.

It may be recalled from chapter 1 of this work that Charles August Siess was a blacksmith and wagon-maker in the village of Highland Park in 1882, and that in the economic depression of 1893 his business, along with thousands of others throughout the United States, failed. Remnants of the Siess family were among those who, as they had in the nineteenth century, lived in households consisting of a married couple and one or more of their children and/or some other blood-related relatives. As early as 1910, Fred Siess, W. Siess, and Henry Siess, all of whose occupations were listed as "machinists," were boarding at 143 Highland Avenue.[24] Throughout the period in which the Model T was produced in the Crystal Palace, that is from 1910 through 1927, families like the Siess family, in neighborhoods like the one that the Siess family lived in, continued to live in households wherein the composition remained essentially unchanged, while the demographic transformation wrought by the need of the automotive industry for fresh workers, created neighborhoods in which the vast majority of the residents were boarders.

In the comparatively brief period between 1900 and 1920 the population of Highland Park increased dramatically, and almost all of the growth in the size of the population was the direct result of expanding labor needs in the Crystal Palace. In 1900 there were 427 inhabitants, but by 1910 that number had increased to 4,120, an increase of 846.9%. By 1914 village officials estimated the population to be 22,000, and the special census taken by the Bureau of the Census on November 15, 1915, counted 27,170 persons claiming residence in Highland Park. According to the last decennial census (1920) taken before the Model T assembly lines in the Crystal Palace were silenced, 46,499 persons were living in the city.[25] Most of the residents of Highland Park were "native white Americans" who, for at least part of the Model T era, lived in households much like those in enumeration district (Zunz-square) number 7.

The rapid rate at which the population of Highland Park increased, along with austerity policies resulting from World War I, and the economic depression of the early 1920s, all contributed to a perennial housing shortage in the city. Despite warnings from Ford Motor Company executives and managers that "[e]mployees should not sacrifice their family rights, pleasures and comforts, by filling the house with roomers and boarders, nor endanger their children's morals or welfare by allowing them to associate with people about whom they know little or nothing,"[26] boarding continued to be the primary response to the housing needs of the Crystal Palace workforce.

Selected at random from within Z-square number 7, and therefore assumed to be typical of households taking in boarders in 1910, was a house on La Belle Avenue where a 44-year-old German male head of household gave his occupation as house decorator, living with his 46-year-old wife, a dressmaker who worked at home. This couple had three school-age children: an 8-year-old boy and two daughters, aged 8 and 13. Eight unmarried auto workers ranging in age from 17 to 36, including one who was the nephew of the head of household, boarded in this home.[27]

Another typical household among those taking in boarders was found on Pasadena Avenue. In this home a 40-year-old man employed as an electrician in "the automotive factory," lived with his 29-year-old wife, whose occupation was listed as boarding housekeeper, and their five-year-old son and three-year-old daughter. Five boarders lived in this home: two were 18 years old, one of whom was an electrician and the other a machinist; also among the boarders, were a 21-year-old clerk and two automotive assemblers, aged 20 and the other 22.[28]

In addition to living in private homes, boarders also lived in establishments that were operated especially for boarders. One such abode on Pasadena Avenue was operated by three sisters, Josephine, Carrie, and Hattie, aged 63, 50, and 47, respectively; their boarding house served as home for 13 lodgers, all of whom worked at the "auto factory," which no doubt was the Crystal Palace.[29]

By themselves, the glimpses into the Siess household on Highland Avenue, and the family homes on La Belle and Pasadena that took in boarders, and the boarding house operated by the three aging sisters, do not tell much about the quality of life in Highland Park. However, when combined with other evidence, such as the work of scholars like Chen-Nan Li, and activist scholar-novelists such as Upton Sinclair, and records such as those maintained by the Sociological Department of the Ford Motor Company, it is possible to construct a profile of the Model T cohort of Ford workers who lived in Highland Park.

Li spent the summer of 1925 working in the Crystal Palace, and during his tenure in the plant, he recorded certain information and impressions about the lives of certain workers employed in the plant. According to Li's observations, the workers lived under all sorts of conditions, ranging from indecent to refined extravagance. In general, it appeared that the workers maintained a reasonably high standard of living. While it may be argued that it is impossible to characterize the average employee in the Crystal Palace, Li's description of the "average Ford man" is, nevertheless, instructive.

According to Li, in 1925 an average Ford man and his family were well fed, consuming three balanced, substantially plentiful meals each day. When dressed in street attire, the worker looked like the average American businessman. An average Ford man was between 35 and 40 years of age.[30] He had a wife who was only slightly younger than he was and who had given birth to two or three children.[31] Apparently, the average wife worked hard at housekeeping and frequently acquired a "good income" by taking in roomers and boarders.[32] The Ford worker was likely to own his house, or have been buying it on installment contract; if he did not own his own house, he probably rented an entire flat consisting of several rooms. In either case, the worker was likely to have had "sufficient" space for his family, and one or two rooms that were rented. If the house or flat was in Highland Park, the room or rooms were quite probably rented to a fellow employee at the Crystal Palace. The house, of course, was supplied with water, gas, electricity, and other modern conveniences. Among the workers' household furnishings, carpets, davenports, and comfortable chairs are likely to have been found, along with a few books and a few pictures on the walls. The worker may also have had a victrola or a piano, a telephone, and perhaps a radio. Many would own a car, most probably a Model T Ford, which was driven to work.[33]

Most of the workers were married, but many were not. The average unmarried worker was most likely to be between 23 and 28 years of age. If he lived in Highland Park, he and at least one other unmarried Ford worker would probably have shared a rented room in a house or apartment. The room would have cost each worker $3.00-$4.00 a week. The unmarried worker was likely to take his meals in a restaurant at a cost of $1.00 to $1.30 per day. Generally, whether married or single in 1925, the worker who was employed in the Crystal Palace appeared to maintain a fairly high standard of living.[34]

Agent-investigators of Ford's Sociological Department, especially from c.1914 to 1917, were prominent figures in the lives of many of those employed in the Crystal Palace. The investigators often had with them a set of instructions for the workers, which covered such issues as cleanliness, sobriety, health, etc. Many workers resented the intrusion of the investigator, even while they appear to have benefited from his intervention. Clearly, improved status within the Crystal Palace through participation in the profit-sharing plan could not compensate for the violation of privacy. A little song that some workers sang seems to capture the mood frequently expressed, and it suggests that there was indeed a great deal of ambivalence toward the company investigator:

> Who is the guy
> That asks you why
> Your money is all spent,
> and quiz——es you

and wif———ey too
About e-nor-mous rent?

Who counts the kids
and lifts the lids
To see that things are clean,
And sure he'll say
Most an-y day
Your bank book must be seen.

In—ves—ti—gator
In—ves—ti—gator
The greatest man you really
    ever knew.

In—ves—ti—gator
In—ves—ti—gator
He starts the rocks a-piling up
    for you.[35]

The quality of life of those who worked in the Crystal Palace, whose "good life" and high standard of living had become the hallmark for the industry, and who had been the envy of automotive workers throughout the United States, had deteriorated drastically by 1929. The description of the conditions experienced by one worker in 1929 was in many ways typical of those who had been employed in the Crystal Palace. The laid-off worker stated, "After 14 years and 3 months of the best endeavor for the Ford Motor Company, I with thousands of others have been sent home." The worker continued, "By economy I have a comfortable home nearly paid for. The rental of a few rooms supply most necessities. I don't think we shall need any help from the community fund, but unless the factories open up before long, there will surely be dire sufferings in Detroit."[36] This worker had not foreseen the wrath of the Great Depression, wherein all but the most fortunate Ford workers, along with millions of other workers, would indeed suffer.

All of the workers of the Model T cohort were pioneers in a new industrial age, whether they were among the relatively few blacks, the large number of ethnics who would soon be "Americanized," or the native white Americans whose social mobility, consciousness and differentiation were accelerated by the profit-sharing plan. Their lives, therefore, enriched the lives of other workers who would follow them. Workers, who having heard the kindhearted, ethnocentric, paternalistic pronouncements and homilies of the king (Henry Ford), and having seen the lights go out in the Crystal Palace while listening to the voices of those in the foundries, in the paint shops, and on the assembly lines, understood more fully, and without any doubt, the need to organize.

Conclusion

Even before the Highland Park plant was fully operational, Ford was thinking about expanding the company. Motivated by the inadequacies of the Highland Park plant, the scarcity of raw materials during the war, and unacceptable vulnerability to the inconsistencies of suppliers, Henry Ford was "projecting bigness in a new and more intensive form than any of his contemporaries had achieved." The basic element in his conception was that the flow of materials and the strategic location of his plant were essential in order for the iron, lumber, water power, coal, rivers and railroads, power plants, foundries, and assembly units to come together in one place, under one management. Thus, Ford and his engineers envisioned a gigantic system that "included control of raw materials, control of their transportation to and from the plant, space for all the chief units they might desire, and close interrelationship among such units. They could then command flow throughout the entire manufacturing cycle, and make bigness creative not only in its separate parts, but as a whole."[1] By 1915 he was ready to begin the creation of a "new and superior type of industry," and he instructed his real estate agent to secretly purchase options on approximately two thousand acres of land on the River Rouge that would become the site of the plant that "symbolized a new industrial era" as the proud home of the first moving assembly line was passing."[2]

Designed by Albert Kahn, the first building in the Rouge complex, the 1,702-foot-long Eagle Boat Building (the B building), was completed in 1917. After the war, the building was converted to vehicle assembly; and Kahn—by now making use of less concrete and more steel—went on to design a powerhouse, byproducts factory, glass plant, foundry, cement plant, open hearth building, coke ovens, and numerous other structures. As stated by David L. Lewis, with its clerestories and butterfly roof, encased in a simple, efficient envelope, the Rouge plant answered all the problems of structure, light, and ventilation. In terms of Kahn's career and architectural history, as Lewis noted, the glass plant stands out. Kahn's biographer, Grant Hildebrand, in 1974 described it as the "single factory that carried industrial architecture forward more than any others," and "probably has as much right to the term [revolutionary] as any other building of the twentieth century." Clearly, as the *New York Times* in 1970 stated in summing up Kahn's work at the Rouge, the plant "is one of the most important structures in the history of architecture, in its functional, rather than its formalist sense."[3] Production at the new and expanding plant on the Rouge River was accompanied by a purge of Model T management and a restructuring of the workforce.

The purge was ongoing, and was methodical and complete as the transfer of operations to the new plant. "From the minute Sorensen moved from Dearborn to the Rouge he was chief engineer as well as production manager," and he and Harry Bennett supervised the brutal purge. Evidently, Sorensen now identified the Rouge with the Model A and Highland Park with the Model T, and was heard scornfully saying, "That's a Model T Idea," and "That's Model T thinking." He told Klann, "We want to fire every Model T son-of-a-bitch!" Klann reported: " 'Charlie, what are you? You worked on the job yourself, too, didn't you?' Sorensen ignored the thrust. Klann's reply may have made his own discharge a certainty."[4]

When Peter E. Martin came down to the Rouge, Sorensen's assistant, Mead L. Bricker, was sent up to the Crystal Palace as superintendent. After assessing the situation, he began to fire some employees himself. Bricker told Klann, "You know those fellows better than I do," and therefore instructed Klann to fire others as their activities were transferred to the Rouge. Klann later pointed out, "They didn't want the supervision to come [from Highland Park] to the Rouge plant." At the same time, some men who went to the Rouge found that they had no jobs there, or that they had been demoted; some of them then quit the Ford Motor Company. Klann, who did much of the firing and was then himself fired, was kept on until the final assembly was moved to the Rouge. Among the top officials who were discharged, or who appraised the situation and left, were Clarence W. Avery, Robert E. Burns, August Degner, Fred Diehl, John Findlater, Charles Hartner, Herbert L. Leister, and I.B. Scofield. Kanzler had resigned in 1926, and Ryan, the sales manager, departed late in 1927. Perhaps more important than the exodus of the upper echelon of the white-collar elites was the weeding out of their abler subordinates. As Nevins notes, "Hundreds of these were dropped, and their disappearance left the company dangerously thin in experienced supervisors and expert workers at a time when the new car was about to demand a miracle in the speedup of production."[5]

While the first generation of the managerial class was being displaced by the purge and the second generation stepped forward to take the reins of production in the Rouge plant, a combination of related conditions worked to redefine the racial composition of the blue-collar workforce: 1) the expansion of the Ford Motor Company that was accelerated by Ford's wartime production, 2) the shortage of labor related to the war and the migration of black workers to the automotive belt, 3) Henry Ford's benevolent disposition toward "Negro workers," and 4) Ford's ongoing battle against organized labor, and the failure of labor to embrace black workers.

According to Nevins and others, Henry Ford had a firm conviction that the races should labor as partners, "the colored man at one end of the log, and the white man at the other." "Still more important, he held that merit, not color, should govern promotion; and Edsel and he made Sorensen and Martin support their position. The result was that at a time when practically all large industries paid grudging attention to skilled and semi-skilled Negroes, and almost none would give a foremanship or white-collar position to a colored person, Ford practiced real equality." According to this same perspective, at the Rouge plant blacks got the same wages and chances as all other employees; black foremen gave orders to whites and blacks alike, and two or three blacks had the authority to challenge the plant superintendent on questions of discrimination. In short, asserted Nevins, the Rouge was the only plant in the industry where blacks shared in all the manufacturing operations.[6]

Ford's willingness to employ black workers may be explained, in part, by his earlier experience of working with William Perry. "One day in 1914 Henry Ford had led an old-time Negro friend, William Perry, with whom he had often manned a crosscut saw during his farming years, into the Highland Park plant, explained some of the machinery, and bade the superintendent to 'see to it that he's comfortable.'"[7] Hence, as legend has it, Perry became the first Negro employee. Within about six years after the war there were more than five thousand blacks working for Ford; the vast majority of them worked at the Rouge plant. By 1926, ten thousand or more blacks represented nearly a tenth of those employed by Ford. It has been estimated that during the open-shop era, the Ford Motor Company employed well over half of all blacks in the motor industry. Ford's success in employing blacks was facilitated by the efforts of the Reverend R.L. Bradby of the Second Baptist Church and the Reverend Everard W. Daniel of St. Matthews Episcopal Church, who helped them find capable men and mediate differences. D.J. Marshall, one of the Episcopalian parishioners, became a leading "Negro-relations" agent for the company from 1923 until his death some twenty years later.[8]

Olivier Zunz has pointed out that Ford's "record" regarding the employment of black workers must be judged carefully. Admittedly, "Ford was the only employer in the city who initiated a new policy in 1919 employing Blacks in all hourly wage classifications, and the only employer to develop openly a hiring network among Blacks in Detroit" through the offices of Reverends Bradby and Daniels. "But this new policy toward Blacks," cautioned Zunz, "spectacular as it might have appeared, had only a limited impact on the sociological composition of the Black community, since most other employers continued to employ Blacks in backbreaking jobs that the whites did not want, such as those in the metal trade industry where the work was hot and dirty."[9]

To a large extent, this research has been an attempt to build a bridge between knowledge of the old and the new, between the Crystal Palace and the Rouge plant, between the appearance of the first cohort of the new manager class and those who succeeded them. It has grown out of a body of scholarship calling for studies giving primary consideration to the underclass employed in the automotive empire.[10] These are workers whose stories are hidden in a maze of industrial records and reports; stories of fingers, hands, and eyes lost while working on an assembly line; stories found in the epitaphs on grave stones marking premature deaths due to "hazards of the job"; stories of racial and ethnic, age and gender discrimination under the guise of "scientific management"; they are, above all else, stories of a few successes, and many more disappointments in pursuit of the American dream. The primary aim of this research has been to begin an analysis of how Ford's production, employment, and personnel policies concerning the production of the Model T in the Crystal Palace affected the quality of life of the average worker, the city of Highland Park, and adjacent communities.

In order to lend a degree of cohesiveness to this study, and to suggest directions for future studies of the underclass of industrial wage-earners, the definition of the quality of life was selected with great care. The definition is based on the assumption that QOL studies should focus on the relationship between the conditions of life and how those conditions are experienced by a particular population; in this case, that particular population is the cohort of workers employed in the Crystal Palace to build the Model T Ford. Throughout this research the definition has guided the decisions about the level of analysis, what kind of data to look for, etc.[11]

Owing to a widely recognized scarcity of accessible historical data, and the associated prohibitions, studies taking the direction of this research are relatively few in number. Not unexpectedly, then, this research has been hampered by several familiar data problems: 1) Traditionally, the underclass has not written autobiographies, and their lives have not been especially inspiring to biographers or other writers; 2) On February 8, 1951, critically important census reports were destroyed by fire in the State of Michigan Archives; 3) Microfilmed copies of some issues of the *Highland Park Times* are available, but segments of the film are unuseable, and the remaining fragments of the original newsprint are so poorly preserved that they crumble at the touch; and 4) most debilitating of all, "The Sociological Department folded and its records were burned after Reverend Dr. Samuel S. Marquis, its head, resigned on January 25, 1921."[12] Each of these is a major obstacle; yet enough data are available to support a study such as this one.

Beginning with a brief narrative of the major event unfolding in Highland Park before the construction of the Crystal Palace, it was noted that before Henry Ford arrived to manufacture the Model T, Captain William H. Stevens had been the most influential individual in determining the direction of development in the area.[13] The really big event, though, was the creation of the world's first automated manufacturing and assembly system, which evolved to make production of the Model T more efficient; a series of related developments had wide-ranging effects throughout the industry, and in the neighborhoods and cities in the vicinity of the Crystal Palace. Major effects resulted from innovations in automotive engineering, machine-tool technology, and the rationalization of production in accordance with the principles of "scientific management." Along with the innovations in design and manufacturing came a new system of personnel management, which depended upon the creation of a new breed of managers, indeed a new class. While revolutionary innovations were being implemented in the Crystal Palace, the effects were being felt elsewhere, but nowhere more than in the neighborhoods nearby the automotive plants.

Among the immediate results of the production, employment, and managerial innovations in the Crystal Palace was the demographic transformation of Highland Park and its vicinity. The demand for labor resulted in an enormous increase in the population, and a disturbance in the male/female ratio of the area. Young, unmarried males were numerically dominant in the restructured population and represented a strain on the social fabric of the region. The imbalance in Detroit was greater than in the nation as a whole, and proportionally even greater in Highland Park and the vicinity of the Crystal Palace. Moreover, it was observed that a few enumeration districts accounted for the most phenomenal aberration in the demographic transformation of Highland Park.[14] It is evident that a more thorough study of the enormous "surplus" of immigrant males and the practice of lodging and boarding is essential to a full understanding of the consequences of the demographic transformation of the quality of life experienced by the Model T cohort of Ford workers.

In the course of outlining major changes in the quality of life experienced in Highland Park before 1930, a number of important, challenging and controversial conclusions have been posited. For example, it has been argued that with regard to its size, its self-consciousness, and the degree of specialization, the *manager class* that appeared as an element in the production of the Model T was unprecedented. Thus, as a key factor in the Crystal Palace, this new class became an important factor in labor and industrial relations, as well as in social relations defined by work and job responsibilities in the Crystal Palace, Highland Park, and throughout the entire industry. In the process, the Ford Motor Company set the pattern in which this new manager class would become entrenched in every sector in industry and manufacturing in the United States. Moreover, it has been argued that contrary to the standard interpretation that sees skilled workers replaced by immigrants who were attracted to the Crystal Palace by superior wages and working conditions, the present analysis strongly suggests that skilled workers were supplanted by the manager class, almost none of whom were of the "immigrant type."

Another conclusion challenging the conventional interpretation that urban deterioration associated with the automotive industry began in the 1960s is that the pattern of deterioration in Highland Park, when compared with the "deindustrialization" described in 1982 by Barry Bluestone and Bennett Harrison, suggests that in 1927 (the end of the Model T era) Highland Park may have been the earliest case of a city declining rapidly as a result of the decision of a major automotive company to relocate a primary manufacturing facility.

Regarding the employment of black workers, this research has noted the previously unnoticed fact that Ford had at least two different policies in hiring, one for the Crystal Palace and another for the Rouge plant.[15] Only a few blacks were employed in the Crystal Palace. The realization that the Ford Motor Company's reputation for hiring black workers did not apply to its practices in Highland Park necessitated an important change in the research strategy. Initially, in deciding to analyze the quality of life, (following the conventional assumption that Ford was the industry leader in the employment of black workers), it had been assumed that a sufficiently large black population would be found in Highland Park and the Crystal Palace to provide a basis against which to compare and contrast the majority of workers in the Crystal Palace with the residents of Highland Park. Since so few blacks lived in Highland Park during the early stages of the Model T era, the larger community of black Detroit was used as a contrast for the quality of life in the Palace and Highland Park. Generally speaking, it was found that the quality of life experienced in the larger community was worse than that found in Highland Park. This reality was especially evident in the quality and conditions of residential housing.

Rather than helping to achieve the conditions Ford believed were essential to good living conditions and efficient work, Ford hiring practices sometimes contributed to making conditions worse. Some of these conditions could have been avoided by hiring more women, and thereby achieving the balance thought to be essential to good home conditions and the creation and maintenance of an efficient workforce.

There is no doubt that when contrasted with the quality of life experienced with earlier settlers, the quality of life among the third and fourth cohorts of Highland Park was radically different. Most of the differences can be attributed to the influence of the Ford Motor Company. For many residents of the Model T cohort, the quality of life was decidedly inferior. Among the company initiatives aimed at improving the living conditions and efficiency in production, programs for upgrading the home and housing conditions, the Americanization of workers, and minimizing the risk of injury in the workplace were prominent. Generally speaking, the evidence suggests that Ford's commitment to the improvement of the QOL of workers was honest and well intended, but the results of its various efforts were often mixed. In the same sense that Ford's efforts were based on the assumption that an improved QOL was essential to the achievement of optimal efficiency in production, policies aimed at improving the QOL of its workers were self-serving.[16] Whatever advantages accrued to the Model T workers, they were often achieved at the expense of privacy, autonomy, and perhaps even dignity and self-esteem.

Throughout this study, a major concern has been to identify sources of data and to elaborate a strategy that will permit the longitudinal analysis of quality of life issues within a particular population and to encourage further study of the Crystal Palace and Highland Park. As this research suggests, such further study could profitably consider: 1) A comparison can be made with some other city in the region—Hamtramck would be an especially good choice for such a comparison; 2) With the present groundwork completed, it is now reasonable to look meaningfully into a wider data base, including church and court records, birth, marriage, and death certificates, etc. It is hoped that this beginning will help to bring forth personal and family data such as genealogical, biographical, and autobiographical information. A 1987 interdisciplinary study by a team of experts has shown that, on a series of indicators selected to demonstrate the "uneven development" of regions within the Detroit area, Highland Park stood out as one of the most rapidly deteriorating suburbs of the region. This book, *Detroit: Race and Uneven Development*, confirms the assertion that Highland Park deserves more attention.[17]

Appendix A
Toward a Statistical Portrait of Model T Workers

The statistical tables in the Appendix, along with those found throughout the text, reveal a portrait of a diverse and rapidly changing cohort of Ford's Model T workers. The portrait shows clearly that the number of workers employed increased rapidly, that their productivity increased, that the Highland Park plant became less prone to "turnover," and that the workplace became increasingly stratified in terms of skill and wages.

Table A.1
Years of Service in The Crystal Palace
for 45,351 Workers as of April 25, 1925

Years of Service	Number of Workers
Less than 1 year	5,412
1	5,523
2	9,492
3	5,773
4	1,379
5	3,880
6	3,842
7	2,121
8	1,349
9	2,603
10	1,878
11	822
12	898
13	389
14	162
15	123
16	56
17	28
18	19
19	6
20	5

Source: Ford Motor Company Archive (FMCA), Accession 40 Box 16. Note: FMCA Accession 62-2, Box 37 shows that as of October 29, 1921 there were 636 women employed in the Crystal Palace; 554 of them apparently worked in the factory, while 82 were designated as office employees.

147

Table A.2
Worker Productivity for the Model T:
Monthly Average 1909-1913

Year	Cars Mfg.	Number of Workmen	Productivity	Index
1909	1,059	1,548	.70	100
1910	1,704	2,573	.66	94
1911	3,483	3,733	.93	133
1912	6,923	6,492	1.07	152
1913	15,284	13,667	1.12	160

Source: FMCA/Accession 922, "Model T Production Statistics." The monthly statistics for men on roll was averaged for each year. A similar table appears in Meyer's *Five Dollar Day*.

Table A.3
Day Wages in the Ford Motor Company c. 1910

Occupation	Number	Percent	$Range	Mean Wage
Foremen	9	6	3.00-7.00	5.01
Mechanics:				
High Skilled	40	28	1.75-5.20	3.90
Skilled	37	26	2.50-4.00	3.15
Laborers	49	34	1.25-3.00	2.48
Miscellaneous	8	6	2.00-3.00	2.59
Total	143	100		

Source: FMCA/Accession 940 Box 18, "An eight-page sample of occupations from about 1910." A version of this table appears in Meyer, 1982:48.

Table A.4
Number and Percent of Ford Workers by Occupation 1913

Occupation	Number	Percent
Operators	6,749	51
Skilled Operators	3,431	26
Unskilled: laborers, helpers, & youth	2,709	21
Mechanics & Subforemen	329	2
Total	13,404	100

Source: Oliver J. Abell, "Labor Classified on a Skill-Wage Basis," *Iron Age* 93 (January 1914), 48; and E.A. Rumley, "Ford's Plan to Share Profits," *World's Work*, 27 (April 1914), 665-66; also, Stephen Meyer, *The Five Dollar Day*, 50.

Table A.5
Ages of 44,519 Employees
in The Crystal Palace as of April 25, 1925

Age	Number
Under 18	733
18-25	7036
25-30	8834
30-35	7527
35-40	7854
40-45	5393
45-50	3190
50-55	1909
55-60	1142
60-65	547
65-70	226
70-75	64
75-80	20
80-85	4

Source: FMCA/Accession 40, Box 16. Note: Under 50 years of age, there were 40,407 employees, and there were 3,192 over 50. Employees under 18 were Trade School Boys and special students. A January 1916 report showed the average as 30.89, with a mode of 25 and a median of 30. This report also stated that the youngest employee was 16, and the oldest 76 (See FMCA/Accession 62, Box 59).

Table A.6
Vote on New Charter by Wards
June 25, 1918

Ward	Yes	No	Percentage Yes	Percentage Ethnic
1	2439	102	95.6	53.5
2	1295	64	95.0	47.3
4	2242	117	95.0	48.1
8	1916	128	93.7	54.0
10	1855	186	90.9	55.9
6	1816	189	90.6	52.8
17	2748	350	90.2	61.0
21	1941	194	90.1	56.1
14	2548	281	90.1	63.0
19	1628	194	89.3	63.0
12	1557	217	87.8	64.0
15	1759	267	86.8	59.8
16	1963	313	86.2	74.7
3	1124	216	83.9	65.5
18	840	200	80.7	78.2
5	751	208	78.3	72.6
13	1180	350	77.0	76.9
7	415	133	75.7	68.2
11	913	313	74.4	81.0
9	896	337	72.6	81.9
20	582	228	71.8	75.2
Detroit	32690	4587	87.7	64.0

Source: Fragnoli, 1982: Table III, page 403.

Appendix B

Origins, Definitions, and Indicators:
A Commentary on the Study of the Quality of Life

There are four issues around which the following commentary revolves. The first concerns the intellectual origins of quality of life (QOL) research and the relationship of earlier developments to the study of the social history of the Crystal Palace and Highland Park's first cohort of automotive workers. Second, there is the problem of defining the QOL in a way that serves as a methodological guide, and that allows for the systematic and consistent comparison of factors defining the QOL across a wide variety of temporal and spatial domains. There are also questions arising out of the current debates in QOL and Social Indicators (SI) research about the measurement of the QOL that have a bearing on this research. Finally, there is the fundamental issue regarding the extent to which the selection of indicators aimed at measuring the QOL is determined by current urban policy issues. What follows here is an attempt to locate the present study within the context of these concerns as they relate to the study of social history.

The intellectual origins of historical demography, or what has more recently been termed Social Indicators of Quality of Life research, is deeply rooted in the past. J. Dennis Willigan and Katherine A. Lynch in their *Sources and Methods of Historical Demography* have shown that modern QOL scholarship may be traced back to three main sources that include scholars who may be characterized as 1) methodologists, 2) political arithmeticians, and 3) theorists.[1]

Epitomized by the work of John Gruant (1620-87), the methodologists were often brilliant mathematicians who attempted to reveal patterns of changes in the composition, density, and mortality of populations. Inspired mainly by the demand of governments for information upon which borrowing and taxation policies could be based, methodologists concentrated on attempting to describe and predict the size of populations. The most immediate intellectual beneficiaries of Gruant's work, namely, Christian Huygens (1620-99), Johan Hudde (1628-1704), and John Dewitt (1625-1672), were public administrators in Holland who developed the first modern life tables which were published in the *Natural and Political Observations* (c. 1671). One of the important dimensions of the work of methodologists is that they showed how birth, baptismal, and burial records could be used to construct life tables (i.e., predictions of life expectancy); their work was, and in fact remains, the conceptual and methodological basis for much of the contemporary QOL/SI research.

The political arithmeticians, among whom the Englishman William Petty (1623-87) is best known, took a quantum leap beyond the methodologists.[2] First, they expanded their data collection to regions outside their own localities. Secondly, and perhaps most importantly, not only were they interested in the size, density, male to female ratio, and the age mix of populations, but they also began within given populations to research the relationship of variations to occupation, the number of households, location, etc. Moreover, what most distinguished the political arithmeticians from their predecessors was their firm belief that their knowledge about "population variables" would allow governments to govern better; that is to say, knowledge of the population variables allowed for control over the population and its resources. In the same sense that Gruant and others provided the foundations of the methodology for QOL research, the research of Petty and Baron de Montyon (1733-1820) established the notion that statistical data on populations could be used to "manipulate" and control the population; and they did so while reinforcing and refining the methodological foundations. It is interesting to note that the "population variables" outlined by Petty and de Montyon are similar to the variables reported in the U.S. Census reports.

Theorists, most notably Thomas Robert Malthus (1766-1834) and Karl Marx 1818-83), were those who were apparently somewhat less concerned about the formal aspects of the mathematics and methodology and more interested in developing grand theories about the relationship of population to the use and distribution of resources. Malthus, of course, argued that while population increased geometrically, production increased arithmetically; hence, the inevitable result (famine) would be that population would grow beyond the capacity of resources essential to its support. It was from Malthus's work that the great population con-

troversy arose, the gist of which was that the survival of human-
ity could be insured if moral restraint was used in an effort to
reduce the birth rate. The importance of Malthus's work is that it
spawned a widely held belief that the size of populations can, and
should, be controlled.

Marx's work (*Grundrisse* 1857-58) is equally important in that
it argued that Malthus's analysis was ahistorical and incorrect.
Looking at the population problem from a historical perspective,
Marx argued that the size of the population was related to the rate
of capital accumulation; specifically, he asserted that the proletariat reproduced itself more rapidly than other classes because
mortality was higher among the proletariat owing to the demand
for child labor, etc. The essential point here is that capitalism,
according to Marx, was the main source of class inequality, and
that inherent in the institutions of capitalism were the seeds of
social inequality, i.e., inequalities in the distribution of the means
for supporting an optimum QOL.

Finally, what is important about the methodologists, political
arithmeticians, and theorists is that traces of their work are apparent in modern QOL research. Ferdinand P. Braudel (1902-1985),
for example, at the time of his death was one of the most influential historians of the twentieth century and the foremost author
among a group of scholars known as the Annales group. Like
their predecessors, the Annales group is distinguished by an
interdisciplinary perspective that combines the knowledge and
methods of such diverse disciplines as demography, ethnography,
economics, geography, psychology, politics, and folklore. Moreover, these scholars have applied their findings to the political
and economic circumstances (QOL factors) in their communities,
and they attempt to universalize their thinking.

Contemporary QOL/SI scholarship has regenerated many of
the same questions raised by Graunt, Petty, Malthus, et al. Within
a growing body of scholarly QOL/SI literature that has a bearing
on the intellectual and methodological issues of this study the
U.S. Environmental Protection Agency's *Quality of Life*; Studies in
Environment, vol. 2; Ben-Cheih Liu's work, especially "Quality of
Life: Concept, Measure and Results";[3] and David A. Larson and
Walton T. Wilford, "The Physical Quality of Life: A Useful Social
Indicator," are particularly important. What follows is a brief dis-
cussion of these and a few related studies.

Commenting on the state of the art of QOL and SI research in
1972, the authors of the EPA-sponsored study noted that the

"anticipation of the need for a new kind of information (i.e., social indicators) could be traced to attempts to assess and react to the impact of Sputnik—the first orbiting satellite launched by the USSR in 1958."[4] The orbiting of Sputnik was seen as evidence that the United States had fallen behind the USSR in an area of techno-logical development vital to United States interests. Faced with the task of catching up, and the apparent lack of a wide range of social statistics that could serve as a basis for the development of a national catchup strategy, the federal government commissioned noted anthropologist Margaret Mead to devise a "social indica-tors" index. The dual purpose of the SI index was to gauge the impact of Sputnik on American society and to provide a scale against which the success of catchup programs could be evaluated.

Beginning with the pioneering work of Mead, tremendous strides were made in the development of a social indicators index. By 1966, Daniel Bell was calling for refinements. He argued that what was needed was a system of "social accounts" which would broaden our thinking about costs and benefits and would put the philosophy and methods associated with economic accounting into a broader framework. In short, Bell asserted that what was needed was a movement toward the measurement of the utiliza-tion of human resources in our social information areas: "1) the measurement of social costs and net returns of innovations; 2) the measurement of social ills . . . ; 3) the creation of 'performance budgets' in areas of defined social needs . . .; and 4) indicators of economic opportunity and social mobility."[5] In addition to Bell's call for refinements, 1966 witnessed the publication of two studies sponsored by the National Aeronautics and Space Administration (NASA). The first was Bertram Gross's research on social system accounting in the U.S., followed by Raymond Bauer's study, which attempted to judge the impact of the space program on U.S. society.[6]

The second wave of developments in SI research came in the wake of domestic violence in the 1960s. The seminal work included Eleanor B. Sheldon's and Wilbert E. Moore's *Indicators of Social Change: Concepts and Measurements*, which served as the "textbook on the status of economic and sociological research, and provided policy makers with a series of scholarly analytical and theoretical discussions of the demographic, structural, distribu-tive and aggregative features of American society."[7]

Heralding the need for "better social reporting," the Depart-ment of Health, Education and Welfare's widely circulated publication, *Toward a Social Report* (1969), asserted that in the future there would be a need for more "data on the aged, on youth, and on women, as well as on ethnic minorities";[8] data that would not only record objective conditions, "but also how different groups of Americans perceive the conditions in which they find themselves."[9] Also in 1969, Otis Dudley Duncan published an article in which it was argued that progress toward the objectives outlined by the Department of Health, Education and Welfare must depend upon 1) cohorts as the basic unit of analysis, 2) a higher quality of replicative studies, 3) more rigorous procedural steps, 4) greater data exchange among researchers, and 5) more attention to calibration. Moreover, Duncan added that studies on occupational change, environmental pollution, victimization by criminal acts, educational opportunities, mental health, and value changes should be accorded top priority.

Taking up tasks suggested by the Department of Health, Education and Welfare, Duncan, et al., Campbell and Converse, in *The Human Meaning of Social Change* (1972) developed the concept of "indicators for the social psychology of the nation." Whereas earlier studies (Sheldon and Moore for example) had been principally concerned with hard data related to the sociostructural aspects of the nation, Campbell and Converse were more concerned with "softer data" of a more sociopsychological sort that are said to reveal the attitudes, expectations, aspirations, and values of the nation. Campbell and Converse took up some important issues not effectively included in earlier studies; among these issues are questions about time use, measures of community, the meaning of work, alienation, etc. Campbell and Converse's initiatives opened the door for the eclectic EPA symposium.

Fortified by the work of Campbell and Converse, Sheldon and Moore, Duncan and many others, the EPA-sponsored symposium in 1972 succeeded in producing the jointly authored landmark *Quality of Life* (1973), by Kenneth E. Hornback, et al., *Studies in Environment*, vol. 2. Among the important contributions of this study was the classification and assessment of the social indicator factors that had previously appeared in the literature; thus, while providing a statement on the history of QOL/SI research, the symposium outlined the framework within which future scholarship would develop. The operationalized definition of the QOL coming out of the symposium is of particular relevance to the present study of the social history of the Crystal Palace, Highland Park, Michigan, and the Model T cohort of Ford workers.

Based upon the assumption that the definition "should focus on the relation between the conditions of life and how those conditions are experienced" by a particular population, "the QOL is defined as a function of the objective conditions and the subjective attitudes involving a defined area of concern."[10] As defined here, there are six factors and subfactors whose statistical indicators may be used to measure the objective aspects of the QOL. For example, the "economic environment" is a major factor, and its subfactors are income, income distribution, economic security, and work satisfaction; the indicators include wage levels, per capita disposable income, etc. More fully, the factors and subfactors lead to the consideration of the following parameters which take the form of questions:

1. The Social Factor includes demographic issues such as (a) immigration as a force in shaping the demographic profile, (b) household/family size and composition, (c) patterns of birth, marriage and dying, and (d) length of residence.
2. The Economic/Market Factor suggests questions about employment and unemployment, ((b) household disposable income, (c) income support measures, (d) per capita value added manufacture, (e) sources and allocation of public revenue, (f) tax payments, and (g) the relationship of economic status to social mobility.
3. Political Factor issues include questions about (a) the number and distribution of qualified voters, (b) the performance of elected officials on selected issues, (c) political coalitions and affiliations, and (d) patterns of electoral participation.
4. The Health Factor concerns (a) the frequency and distribution of sickness and disease, (b) mortality and life expectancy, (c) medical expenses, and (d) the availability and use of medical care.
5. The Physical Environment Factor considers (a) percent deteriorated housing, (b) overcrowding/1.01 persons per room? (c) value of housing, (d) rental costs, (e) percent owner/renter occupied, (f) plumbing, and (g) location of housing.

Answers, even incomplete answers, to these questions help to explain how residence in Highland Park and employment in the Crystal Palace are related to where "a particular people" fall on a Quality of Life index.

Regarding the decision of which subpopulations are to be analyzed, the work of the symposium is again instructive. Based upon a "brief review" of relevant literature, the symposium concluded that "geographic location, education, age, ethnicity, health, sex, political disposition, socioeconomic status, and life adjustment"[11] were identified as the optimum dimensions along which variations perceptions and attitudes about environmental subfactors may be divided. Since such a definition of the QOL posits both objective conditions and subjective attitudes, it is clear that the population will be subdivided the same way in the measurement of both the objective and the subjective dimensions. Put another way, the definition insists that the same population be studied, rather than one population for the objective component, and another for the subjective.

This point is reiterated because of the subtlety with which the authors of the EPA study moved from a consideration of the literature relevant to perceptions and attitudes about the environmental factor, to the construction of the list of "representative" analytical categories that are to be used in the assessment of the QOL as it is reflected in indicators of both the objective and the subjective reality. Thus, "Using lists of QOL factors as one axis, it is possible to generate a series of QOL matrices, e.g., factors by income matrix, factors by age matrix, etc. Each matrix of data would show the relationship between the factors and one of the population parameters."[12] With the matrices serving as the summation of this commentary thus far, the critical questions—those explored in this research—remain: Is meaningful, systematic study of the history of quality of life possible? If so, what direction should such research take?

Within the boundaries of established QOL/SI scholarship, the historical analysis of the QOL can take either of two paths. Given a QOL factor, and a particular time and place with a specific subset of the population (e.g. Economic Factor/income from wages for work in the Crystal Palace, c. 1910-27, and adult females), one path would be to use normative historical documentation and whatever randomly generated statistics one may find. Given the same set of objective circumstances, another path would be to select indicators that are most uniformly reported over the longest period of time. Ideally, the evidence recorded in a diary or genealogical record can be combined or correlated with statistics reported in census reports, city directories, etc. In such circumstances, the task of the historian is to make the best use of the evidence, moving via the historical narrative form one type of data to another.

In summary, then, the first two decades of modern QOL and SI research may be characterized as having fostered 1) a growing interest in methodological rigor and the recognition of the need to compare and validate various research strategies; 2) an increased emphasis on the development of standardized time series data, and the expansion of the variety of statistics collected by governmental agencies; and 3) the recognition of the need for, and the expanded collection of, subjective data concerning occupational status, time budgets, mental health, political participation, etc. However, in spite of the impressive array of accomplishments outlined in a growing body of literature on both basic and applied SI research, at present there is no unified theory concerning methods or priorities for research.[13] The failure to develop a theoretical and methodological consensus is testimony to the complexities bedeviling SI research—complexities inherent in both the human subject and the nature of the evidence, and which are compounded by the countless, often unclear, motives of SI scholars. But, contrary to H.J. Dyos, who argues that "there can be no reliable historical chart to the quality of urban life without a new discipline for connecting the historical and the literary traditions of scholarship,"[14] here it is argued that innovative applications of the centuries old disciplines of public and applied history are more than adequate.

Notes

Introduction

1. Stephen Meyer III, *The Five Dollar Day: Labor Management and Social Control in the Ford Motor Company 1908-1921* (Albany, New York: State University of New York Press, 1981) 4.

2. Nora Faires, "Assembling the History of Detroit," *Michigan Quarterly Review* (September 1985): 16.

3. Faires 1985, 5.

4. Faires 1985, 5.

5. Sam Bass Warner and Sylvia Fleisch, *Measurement for Social History* (Beverly Hills, California, Sage Press, 1977) 68.

6. David Katzman, *Before the Ghetto: Black Detroit in the Nineteenth Century* (Chicago: University of Illinois Press, 1973); Stephen Thernstrom, *Poverty and Progress: Social Mobility in a Nineteenth-Century City* (Cambridge, Massachusetts: Harvard University Press, 1964); Forrester B. Washington, "The Negro in Detroit: A Survey of Conditions of a Negro Group in a Northern Industrial Center During the War Prosperity Period" (Detroit, 1920).

7. Olivier Zunz, *The Changing Face of Inequality* (University of Chicago Press, 1982) 403.

1. Highland Park Before the Crystal Palace

1. This sketch of early life in Highland Park is based primarily on information given to Ellen Hathaway by members of the Highland Park Historical Society. Many of the charter members of the society were direct descendants of early settlers. What appears to be the original typescript of this information may be found in Highland Park's McGregor Library Museum; there are approximately 120-30 pages in this document but they are not consecutively numbered. This manuscript is hereinafter identified as HPHS.

2. WPA Writer's Project in Michigan, *Michigan: A Guide to the Wolverine State* (1937) 290.

3. WPA, 289-93.

4. HPHS, 1946 passim.

5. HPHS, 1946 passim.

6. HPHS, 1946 passim.

7. HPHS, 1946 passim.

8. HPHS, 1946 passim.

9. HPHS, 1946: passim.

10. HPHS, 1946: passim.

11. HPHS, 1946: passim.

12. HPHS, 1946: passim.

13. HPHS, 1946: passim; WPA, *Wolverine State*, 290.

14. HPHS, 1946: passim.

15. HPHS, 1946: passim.

16. Robert H. Wiebe, *The Search for Order, 1877-1920* (New York: Hill and Wang, 1967) xiii, 1-10.

17. Wiebe, *Search for Order*, 1-10.

18. Wiebe, *Search for Order*, 1-10.

19. For a more complete discussion of the concept and definition of quality of life (QOL), and the rationale behind it, see Appendix B.

2. Frederick Winslow Taylor and Scientific Management

1. Horace Lucien Arnold and Fay Leone Faurote, *Ford Methods and the Ford Shops* (1915; reprint, New York: Arno, 1972) 20 (page citation is to the original edition); Bruce W. McCalley, *Model T Ford: The Car That Changed the World* (Iola, Wisconsin: Krause, 1994); Victor W. Page, *Ford Owner's Handbook of Repair & Maintenance: Models T and A* (Los Angeles: Clymer, 1953).

2. About 600 hundred were assembled at the Highland Park plant and the additional 400 at other Ford facilities.

3. Wiebe, *Search for Order*, 151. Similarly, Henry Eilbirt has observed that there is no evidence of the application of specialization to labor administration before 1900; and that in 1900, there did not yet exist a comprehensive personnel department, as we know it today. See Eilbirt, "The Development of Personnel Management in the United States," *Business History Review* 33 (1959): 345-64.

4. Milton J. Nadworny, "The Origins of the Taylor System," *Scientific Management and the Unions, 1900-1932* (Cambridge: Harvard University Press, 1955) 1-13; Wiebe, *Search for Order*, 151; Eilbirt, "Development of Personnel Management," 345.

5. Eilbirt, "Development of Personnel Management," 347.

6. H.S. Person, "The Origin and Nature of Scientific Management," in *Scientific Management in Industry*, ed. H.S. Person (New York: Harper, 1929) 12.

7. Eilbirt, "Development of Personnel Management," 356.

8. Frederick A. Halsey, "A Premium Plan for Paying Labor," in A.S.M.E. *Transactions* 1891: 755-64.

9. A.S.M.E., *Transactions*, 1895: 856-58.

10. Eilbirt, "Development of Personnel Management," 1-13; Nelson, *Managers and Workers*, 61-68.

11. Frederick Winslow Taylor, *Shop Management* (New York: Harper, 1911).

12. Cited in Person, "The Origin and Nature of Scientific Management," 8; Cited in Nadworny, *Scientific Management and the Unions*, 7.

13. Person, "The Origin and Nature of Scientific Management," 7.

14. Robert Kanigel, "Frederick Taylor's Apprenticeship," *The Wilson Quarterly* 20.3 (1996): 44-45.

Henry L. Gnatt, who first worked with Taylor at Midvale, and later became his chief assistant, and Carl Barth, a mathematician, played important roles in solving many problems, and played the key role in spreading and implementing the "Taylor" idea. The Barth slide rules marked one of the great advances in the Taylor system. Sanford E. Thompson was also among the early insiders who played an important part in the development of the Taylor system; Thompson had extensive training in the building trades and became a specialist in time study. See Interstate Commerce Commission, *Evidence Taken by the Interstate Commerce Commission in the Matter of Proposed Advances in Freight Rates by Carriers*, August to December 1910, 61st Congress, 3rd session (Washington, 1911) 4: 2666-67.

15. Alfred H. Kelly, Winfred A. Harbison, and Herman Belz, *The American Constitution*, 6th ed. (New York: Norton, 1983) 438.

16. Kanigel, "Frederick Taylor," 44-45.

17. Allan Nevins and Frank Ernest Hill, *Ford: The Times, the Man, the Company* (New York: Scribner's, 1954) 468.

18. Nevins, *Ford, The Times*, 474.

19. Nevins, *Ford, The Times*, 468.

20. Nevins, *Ford, The Times*, 468-69.

21. Nevins, *Ford, The Times*, 469.

22. Frederick Winslow Taylor, "Testimony Before HR," Scientific Management (New York: Harper, 1947) 27.

23. Nevins, *Ford: The Times*, 468.

24. Taylor, "Principles of Scientific Management," *Scientific Management*, 22.

25. Taylor, "Principles of Scientific Management," *Scientific Management*, fn. page 130.

26. Taylor, "Testimony Before HR," *Scientific Management*, 40-41.

27. Taylor, "Testimony Before HR," *Scientific Management*, 42.

28. Taylor, "Testimony Before HR," *Scientific Management*, 44.

29. Taylor, "Testimony Before HR," *Scientific Management*, 44.

30. Keith Sward, *The Legend of Henry Ford* (New York: Russell, 1948) 10.

31. George S. May, *A Most Unique Machine: The Michigan Origins of the American Automobile Industry* (Grand Rapids: Eerdman's, 1975) 107.

32. Joe Blakenbaker, "Ford, Henry," review of *Ford, the Dust and the Glory,* by Leo Levine, in David L. Porter, *Biographical Dictionary of American Sports* (New York: Greenwood, 1988) 9-10.

33. Leo Levine, *Ford: The Dust and the Glory: A Racing History* (New York: Macmillan, 1968).

34. McCalley, *Model T. Ford,* 1.

35. Levine, *Ford,* 6.

36. McCalley, *Model T Ford,* 1.

37. McCalley, *Model T Ford,* 2.

38. James Flink, "Henry Ford and the Triumph of the Automobile," in *Technology in America: A History of Individuals and Ideas,* ed. Carroll W. Pursell (Cambridge: MIT Press, 1990) 180; Levine, *Ford,* 6.

39. Levine, *Ford,* 38.

40. Steve Babson, *Working Detroit: The Making of a Union Town* (New York: Adama Books, 1984) 29.

41. Sward, *Legend of Henry Ford,* 33.

42. Nevins, *Ford,* 451; Henry Ford, *My Life and Work* (Garden City: Doubleday, 1922) 73. Ford stated that it was the best in the "country," but he would not have been wrong in saying, "the world."

43. Nevins, *Ford,* 451-52.

44. David Lewis, "Ford and Kahn," *Michigan History* 64.5 (1980): 21; Ford R. Bryan, *Henry's Lieutenants,* 140.

45. Meyer, *Five Dollar Day,* 3.

46. Bryan, *Ford's Lieutenants,* 140.

47. Nevins, *Ford,* 454.

48. Nevins, *Ford,* 452.

49. Nevins, *Ford,* 453.

50. Bryan, *Henry's Lieutenants,* 140-43. In Detroit alone, in addition to those already mentioned, Kahn's designs include the following: First National Bank Building, Detroit Free Press, Detroit News, Detroit Trust Company, Harper Hospital, Herman Kiefer Hospital, Woman's Hospital, Temple Beth El, Detroit Golf Club, Country Club of Detroit, Detroit Athletic Club, Fisher Building, General Motors Building, New Center Building. Also noteworthy, the Willow Run bomber plant in Ypsilanti, Michigan and the University of Michigan's Hill Auditorium in 1913, the Natural Science Building in 1917, the Central Library in 1919, University Hospital 1920, Angell Hall 1922, and the Medical Building in 1925.

51. Nevins, *Ford,* 452; *Ford Times* January 1910.

52. Quoted in Nevins, *Ford*, 6.

53. Arnold and Faurote, *Ford Methods*, 41.

54. Arnold and Faurote, *Ford Methods*, 97.

55. Arnold and Faurote, *Ford Methods*, 28-29.

56. Arnold and Faurote, *Ford Methods*, 98-99.

57. Fred H. Colvin, "Continuous Pouring in the Ford Foundry," *American Machinist* 39 (1913): 910-12; Arnold and Faurote, *Ford Methods*, 335.

58. Colvin, "Ford Foundry," 910-12; Arnold and Faurote, *Ford Methods*, 356.

59. Arnold and Faurote, *Ford Methods*, 328.

60. Arnold and Faurote, *Ford Methods*, 328.

61. Arnold and Faurote, *Ford Methods*, 34.

62. Meyer, *Five Dollar Day*, 29-30.

63. Horace L. Arnold, "Ford Methods and Ford Shops," *Engineering Magazine* 1914: 510.

64. Fred H. Colvin and Lucian L. Haas, *Jigs and Fixtures*, New York: McGraw-Hill, 1943, 1; Franklin D. Jones, *Jig and Fixture Design*, New York: Industrial, 1920, 1-13; Meyer, *Five Dollar Day*, 26.

65. Arnold, "Ford Methods and Ford Shops," 510.

66. Arnold and Faurote, *Ford Methods*, 102.

67. Fred H. Colvin, "Methods Employed in Making the Ford Magneto," *American Machinist* 39 (1913): 311-16; Arnold, "Ford Methods and Ford Shops," 510.

68. Arnold, "Ford Methods and Ford Shops," 510; Meyer, *Five Dollar Day*, 34.

69. Arnold and Faurote, *Ford Methods*, 206.

70. Ford Motor Company Archives, Oral History Section: "Reminiscences of Max F. Wollering."

71. Arnold and Faurote, *Ford Methods*, 106.

72. Oliver J. Abell, "Making The Ford Motor Car," *Iron Age*, June 1912, 1389; Fred Colvin, "Machining Ford Cylinders," *American Machinist* 38 (1913): 846.

73. Arnold and Faurote, *Ford Methods*, 131.

74. Colvin, "Machining Ford Cylinders."

75. Arnold and Faurote, *Ford Methods*, 105.

76. Arnold and Faurote, *Ford Methods*, 182.

77. Fred H. Colvin, "Forging and Machining Ford Front Axles," *American Machinist* 39 (1913): 189-91; Arnold and Faurote, *Ford Methods*, 193.

78. Ford Motor Company Archives, Oral History Section: "The Reminiscences of John Wondersee."

79. Victor W. Page, *Model T and A Ford Cars* (Los Angeles: Floyd Clymer Publications, 1950) 26; Arnold and Faurote, *Ford Methods*, 135-36.

80. Arnold and Faurote, *Ford Methods*, 139.

81. Page, *Model T Cars*, 26 and 111; Arnold and Faurote, *Ford Methods*, 135-36, 139.

82. Arnold and Faurote, *Ford Methods*, 193.

83. Arnold and Faurote, *Ford Methods*, 102.

84. Arnold and Faurote, *Ford Methods*, 156.

85. Arnold and Faurote, *Ford Methods*, 247.

86. Colvin, "Front Axles," 189-191; Arnold and Faurote, *Ford Methods*, 193-95.

87. Arnold and Faurote, *Ford Methods*, 330.

88. Arnold and Faurote, *Ford Methods*, 359.

89. Arnold and Faurote, *Ford Methods*, 330.

90. Arnold and Faurote, *Ford Methods*, 331.

3. Technological Innovation
and the Demographic Transformation of Highland Park

1. United States Department of Commerce, Bureau of the Census, "Special Census of Highland Park, November 1915."

2. Sam Bass Warner and Sylvia Fleisch, *Measurements for Social History* (Beverly Hills: Sage Press, 1977) 17.

3. Warner and Fleisch, *Measurements for Social History*, 17-18.

4. Warner and Fleisch, *Measurements for Social History*, 20-21.

5. Warner and Fleisch, *Measurements for Social History*, 20-21.

6. Barry Bluestone and Bennett Harrison, *The Deindustrialization of America Plant Closings, Community Abandonment, and the Dismantling of Basic Industry* (New York: Basic Books, 1982).

7. Olivier Zunz, *The Changing Face of Inequality: Urbanization, Industrial Development and Immigration in Detroit, 1880-1920* (Chicago: University of Chicago Press, 1982) 309.

8. Raymond R. Fragnoli, *The Transformation of Reform: Progressivism in Detroit—and After 1912-1933* (New York: Garland, 1982) 8-9.

9. David M. Katzman, *Before The Ghetto: Black Detroit in the Nineteenth Century* (Chicago: University of Chicago Press, 1973) 13.

10. George E. Haynes, *Negro Newcomers in Detroit, Michigan: A Challenge to Christian Statesmanship, A Preliminary Survey* (1918; reprint, New York: Arno Press-*New York Times*, 1969) 7.

11. Henderson H. Donald, "The Negro Migration of 1916-1918," *Journal of Negro History* 6 (1921): 485; Haynes, *Negro Newcomers in Detroit*, 6.

12. Donald, "Negro Migration," 486-87.

13. Haynes, *Negro Newcomers in Detroit*, 7.

14. Glen E. Carlson, "The Negro in the Industries of Detroit" (Ph.D. diss., University of Michigan, 1929) 40, 74-76.

15. Donald, "Negro Migration," 486.

16. William S. Rossiter, *Increase in Population in the United States, 1910-1920* (Washington, D.C.: Government Printing Office, 1922) 128.

17. It may be noted that Rossiter's observations are not consistent with Donald's; Rossiter stated that Michigan's increase was 352 percent, although the increase in number amounted to only 42,000 persons. The disparity is not at issue; whatever the case, the increase was remarkable.

18. Rossiter, *Increase in Population*, 128; David Allan Levine, *Internal Combustion: The Races in Detroit, 1915-1926* (Westport: Greenwood Press, 1976) 44; Detroit Bureau of Government Research, The Negro in Detroit (1926) Section 2, "Population," 15. It should also be noted that the increase in Detroit's population was caused primarily by migration to the city: of 528,000 people added to the population between 1910 and 1920, 412,000 were migrants. Natural increase accounted for 109,000 new inhabitants (with an average birth rate of 32 per 1,000 and a death rate of 15 per 1,000), and annexation of new territory to the city brought only 7,000 new people in to the expanded city limits. See Detroit City Planning Commission, *Master Plan Reports: The People of Detroit* (1946) 5, 11-12; Ticknor, "Motor City," 162; Zunz, *Changing Face of Equality*, 287; Donald, "Negro Migration," 483; see also, W.E.B. DuBois, "The Migration of Negroes," *The Crisis* 14 June 1917: 63-66.

19. While the emphasis here is on black immigrants to the city of Detroit, it should be not be forgotten that their entrance coincided with the influx of other southern workers, generally to Detroit, Pontiac, Lansing, Flint, Saginaw, Toledo, and South Bend—the centers of automobile production. Although the number of blacks increased significantly, it still was a relatively small fraction of the total number of southern migrants who found employment in the automotive industry. That from the beginning of the industry's major expansion, blacks were greatly outnumbered by southern whites was to exert an important bearing on the relation of Negro workers to the industry and to the automobile unions, according to Lloyd H. Bailer, "The Negro Automobile Works," *Journal of Political Economy* 51 (1943): 415.

20. *Detroit News* 2 April 1918.

21. *Detroit News* 25 January 1918.

22. Forrester B. Washington, *The Negro in Detroit: A Survey of Conditions of a Negro Group in a Northern Industrial Center during the War Prosperity Period* (Detroit: Research Bureau Associated Charities of Detroit, 1920); Zunz, *Changing Face of Inequality*, 288.

23. Richard W. Thomas, "The Black Experience in Detroit: 1916-1917," *Blacks and Chicanos in Michigan*, ed. Homer Hawkins and Richard

W. Thomas (Lansing: Michigan Department of State, 1979) 56-57; Haynes, *Negro Newcomers*, 77.

24. Steve Babson, *Working Detroit* (New York: Adama Books, 1984) 23.

25. Sidney Glazer, *Detroit: A Study in Urban Development* (New York: Bookman, 1965) 79.

26. Warner and Fleisch, *Measurements for Social History*, 68.

27. Writers' Program of the Work Projects Administration in the State of Michigan, *Michigan: A Guide to the Wolverine State* (New York: Oxford University Press, 1941) 290.

28. *Highland Parker* 20 February 1920: 4.

29. United States Department of Commerce, Bureau of the Census, Special Census of the Population of Highland Park, Michigan, November 15, 1915.

30. Census Bureau, 1915, Census of Highland Park.

31. Babson, *Working Detroit*, 25.

32. Zunz, *Changing Face of Inequality*, 354.

33. Warner and Fleisch, *Measurements for Social History*, 19.

34. Kingsley Davis and Pietronella van den Oever, "Demographic Foundations of New Sex Roles," *Population and Development Review* 8.3 (1982): 499.

35. Davis and van den Oever, "Demographic Foundations of New Sex Roles," 499.

36. Babson, *Working Detroit*, 24.

37. Chester L. Hunt, "Female Occupational Roles and Urban Sex Ratios in the United States, Japan and the Philippines," *Social Forces* 43 (1965): 412; and Susan E. Bloomberg, et al., "A Census Probe into Nineteenth-Century Family History: Southern Michigan 1850-1800," *Journal of Social History* 5 (1971): 35.

38. Robert W. De Forest and Lawrence Veiller, *The Tenement House Problem* (New York: Macmillan, 1903) 146-47.

39. Warner, Bloomberg et al., "Family History: Southern Michigan," 33.

4. White- and Blue-Collar Workers in the Crystal Palace

1. Olivier Zunz, *Making America Corporate, 1870-1920* (Chicago: University of Chicago Press, 1990) 79.

2. Zunz, *Making America Corporate*, 80.

3. Alfred D. Chandler, *The Visible Hand: The Managerial Revolution in American Business* (Cambridge: Belknap Press Harvard University, 1977) 4.

4. Chandler, *Visible Hand*, 79.

5. Chandler, *Visible Hand*, 3.

6. Chandler, *Visible Hand*, 486.

7. Chandler, *Visible Hand*, 486.

8. Zunz, *Making America Corporate*, 133.

9. Ford R. Bryan, *Henry's Lieutenants* (Detroit: Wayne State University Press, 1993) 214.

10. Bryan, *Henry's Lieutenants*, 214.

11. Charles E. Sorensen, *My Forty Years with Ford* (New York: Norton, 1956) 16.

12. Sorensen, *My Forty Years With Ford*, 117.

13. Bryan, *Henry's Lieutenants*, 215.

14. Bryan, *Henry's Lieutenants*, 267.

15. Bryan, *Henry's Lieutenants*, 155.

16. Bryan, *Henry's Lieutenants*, 16.

17. James J. Flink, "Henry Ford and the Triumph of the Automobile," in *Technology in America*, ed. Carroll W. Pursell, Jr. (Cambridge: MIT Press, 1990) 185.

18. Allan Nevins, Ford; *The Times, the Man, the Company* (New York: Scribner, 1954) 466.

19. Allan Nevins and Frank Ernest Hill, *Ford: Expansion and Challenge, 1915-1933* (New York: Scribner, 1957) 520.

20. Nevins and Hill, *Ford: Expansion*, 354.

21. Gail Cooper, "Frederick Winslow Taylor and Scientific Management," *Technology in America*, ed. Pursell, 164.

22. Zunz, *Making America Corporate*, 5.

23. Sidney Glazer, *Detroit: A Study In Urban Development* (New York: Bookman, 1965) 18.

24. Robert C. Ackerson, "Historiography: Some Milestones in Automotive Literature," *Michigan Quarterly Review* 4 (1980) and 1 (1981): 768.

25. Zunz, *Making America Corporate*, 80.

26. Chandler, *Visible Hand*, 4.

27. Zunz, *Making America Corporate*, 6.

28. Zunz, *Making America Corporate*, 6.

29. Zunz, *Making America Corporate*, 6-9.

30. Zunz, *Making America Corporate*, 9.

31. David Nelson, *Managers and Workers: Origins of The New Factory System in the United States, 1880-1920* (Madison: University of Wisconsin Press, 1975) ix.

32. Peter F. Drucker, "Work and Tools," in *Technology and Culture*, ed. Melvin Kransberg and William H. Davenport (New York: Schocken Books, 1972) cited in Harry Braverman, *Labor and Monopoly Capital: The Degradation of Work in the Twentieth Century* (New York: Monthly Review Press, 1974) 88.

33. Braverman, *The Degradation of Work*, 252.

34. Braverman, *The Degradation of Work*, 65.

35. Braverman, *The Degradation of Work*, 69.

36. Martha Banta, *Taylored Lives: Narrative Productions in the Age of Taylor, Veblen, and Ford* (Chicago: University of Chicago Press, 1993) 4.

37. Banta, *Taylored Lives*, 14.

38. Banta, *Taylored Lives*, 5.

39. Braverman, *The Degradation of Work*, 126.

40. Braverman, *The Degradation of Work*, 113-14.

41. Braverman, *The Degradation of Work*, 326.

42. Braverman, *The Degradation of Work*, 349.

43. Arne Kalleberg and Larry Griffin, "Class, Occupation, and Inequality in Job Rewards," *American Journal of Sociology* 85 (1980): 731-68.

44. Stephen Meyer III, *The Five Dollar Day: Labor Management and Social Control in the Ford Motor Company, 1908-1921* (Albany: State University of New York, 1981) 42-43.

45. Meyer, *Five Dollar Day*, 43.

46. Marquis, *Who Was Who in America*, vol. 8 (Chicago: Marquis Who's Who, 1982-1985) 335; Alberta Lawrence, ed., *Who's Who Among North American Authors*, vol. 5 1931-1932 and vol. 6 1933-34-35 (Los Angeles: Golden Gate, 1932 and 1935) 773, 833.

47. Charles Reitell, "Machinery and Its Effect Upon the Workers in The Automotive Industry," *The Annals of the American Academy of Political and Social Sciences* November 1924: 37.

48. Reitell, "Machinery and Its Effect," 37.

49. Meyer, *Five Dollar Day*, 35-36.

50. Meyer, *Five Dollar Day*, 37-38.

51. Reitell, "Machinery and Its Effect," 39.

52. Meyer, *Five Dollar Day*.

53. Reitell, "Machinery and Its Effect" 39.

54. Reitell, "Machinery and Its Effect," 39.

55. Reitell, "Machinery and Its Effect," 40.

56. According to Emma Rothschild, who is often credited with coining the term, Fordism was the technology of mass assembly-line production made possible by the rapid expansion of output and capital investment. The new technology was based on machinery, and on the rational reorganization of work to fit the rhythm of the new machinery.

Rothschild explained, "In the new organization of auto production, unskilled workers were seen by management as rather simple machines which happened to be alive—Henry Ford expressed this attitude most clearly in his description of factory life: A business is men and machines united in the production of a commodity and both the men and the machines need repairs and replacements. . . . Machinery wears out and needs to be restored. Men grow uppish, lazy or careless." Emma Rothschild, *Paradise Lost: The Decline of the Auto-Industrial Age* (New York: Random House, 1973) 34.

57. Nelson, *Managers and Workers*, 43.

58. Nelson, *Managers and Workers*, 42.

59. Nelson, *Managers and Workers*, 43.

60. Nelson, *Managers and Workers*, 101.

61. Ford Motor Company Archive, Accession 940, Box 18: "Mr. Lee's Talk to the First Group of Investigators, April 15, 1914."

62. Ford Motor Company Archives, Accession 940, Box 16: "Interview with William P. Baxter."

63. Robert Kanigel, "Frederick Taylor's Apprenticeship," *The Wilson Quarterly* 20.3 (1996): 51.

5. From Ethnic Squalor to White-Collar Splendor

1. The black community has been selected as the baseline because it became the majority in the vicinity of the Crystal Palace by about 1930, and because even a casual analysis of the historical record that the experience of the black community was unique in a number of ways.

2. The definition of the quality of life (QOL) is critical to this analysis. Readers may wish to refer to Appendix B for an extensive discussion of this concept.

3. "Swarming Places of Detroit's Poor," *Detroit Free Press* 9 June 1907: Pt. 4.

4. "Detroit's Housing Problem Is a Serious Matter," *Detroit Free Press* 6 November 1910: 3.

5. *Detroit Free Press* 6 November 1910.

6. *Detroit Free Press* 6 November 1910.

7. *Detroit Free Press* 6 November 1910.

8. *Detroit Free Press* 6 November 1910.

9. *Detroit Free Press* 6 November 1910.

10. *Detroit Free Press* 6 November 1910.

11. *Detroit Free Press* 9 June 1907.

12. Regina Koscielski, "Portrait of a Polish-American," *Immigrants and Migrants: The Detroit Ethnic Experience*, ed. David W. Hartman (Detroit: New University Thought, 1974) 114.

13. Koscielski, "Portrait of a Polish-American," 115.

14. Koscielski, "Portrait of a Polish-American," 116.

15. Koscielski, "Portrait of a Polish-American," 116.

16. David Allan Levine, *Internal Combustion: The Races in Detroit, 1915-1926* (Westport: Greenwood Press, 1976) 3.

17. George E. Haynes, *Negro Newcomers in Detroit, Michigan: A Challenge to Christian Statesmanship, a Preliminary Survey* (1918; reprint, New York: Arno Press-*New York Times*, 1969) 21.

18. Levine, *Internal Combustion*, 125.

19. Levine, *Internal Combustion*, 125.

20. David M. Katzman, *Before the Ghetto: Black Detroit in the Nineteenth Century* (Chicago: University of Ilinois Press, 1973).

21. Katzman, *Before the Ghetto*, 74-75.

22. Haynes, *Negro Newcomers*, 22.

23. Haynes, *Negro Newcomers*, 23.

24. Detroit Bureau of Government Research (DBGR), "Negro in Detroit," vol. 5, 10.

25. DBGR, "Negro in Detroit," vol. 4, 5.

26. Levine, *Internal Combustion*, 50-51; *Detroit News Tribune* 4 June 1911.

27. Haynes, *Negro Newcomers*, 21.

28. Haynes, *Negro Newcomers*, 21.

29. The Detroit Board of Health, "Report to the Health Officer on Housing and Health in Detroit," 1911: 9-10.

30. Ford Motor Company Archive, Accession 940, Box 5, "Report on Mayor's Housing Conference."

31. *Pipp's Weekly*, March, April and August, 1928.

32. Levine, *Internal Combustion*, 40.

33. Detroit Board of Commerce, The Americanization Committee of Detroit, *Annual Report*, 31 March 1921: 46, in DPL and MHC/Bentley.

34. *Detroit Free Press* 15 December 1987: 9c.

35. Levine, *Internal Combustion*, 159.

36. Levine, *Internal Combustion*, 3-4, 167-90; Dancy, *Sand Against the Wind*, 21-34; Kenneth T. Jackson, *The Ku Klux Klan in the City 1915-1930* (New York: Oxford University Press, 1967) 27-143; Olivier Zunz, *The Changing Face of Inequality: Urbanization, Industrial Development, and Immigration in Detroit, 1880-1920* (Chicago: University of Chicago Press, 1982) 324.

37. Levine wrote, "On Tuesday morning, September 8, 1925, after telling the police of his intentions, Ossian Sweet moved into the house. There were seven people making the move with him. They were his wife; Henry Sweet, his twenty-one-year-old brother, who was a fourth year student at Wilberforce University; Joseph Mack, Ossian Sweet's chauffeur; Dr. Otis' Sweet, another brother who was a Detroit dentist; William E. Davis, a friend of Otis who was both a pharmacist and a federal narcotics agent; John Latting, a friend of Henry's, also a student at Wilberforce; and Norris Murray, a chauffeur and handyman. Since

school was scheduled to reopen on the fifteenth of September, both Henry Sweet and his friend John Latting expected to leave Detroit within the week. Otis Sweet and William Davis planned to room with the Sweet family for the winter. With the baby Iva, who had been left with her grandparents, it was to be a household of five." See Levine, *Internal Combustion*, 161; Haldeman-Julius, "The Defendants in the Sweet Murder Case," 27, 30-31; Dancy, *Sand Against the Wind*, 23-24; Recorder's Court Detroit, Michigan: "Recorder's Court File no. 60317-60318"; *Detroit City Directory*, 1925-26; Turner and Moses, *Colored Detroit*, 74.

38. Haldeman-Julius, *Clarence Darrow's Two Great Trials*, 32-36; cited in Levine, 162.

39. Levine, *Internal Combustion*, 162.

40. Levine, *Internal Combustion*, 163.

41. Levine, *Internal Combustion*, 163.

42. Levine, *Internal Combustion*, 164.

43. *Detroit Times* 10 September 1925; *Detroit News* 10 September 1925; *Detroit Free Press* 19 November 1925.

44. Levine, *Internal Combustion*, 164.

45. The Sweet trial received international attention, both because of the issues involved, and because Clarence Darrow was the defense lawyer. In the first trial the jurors were unable to reach a verdict; seven of the jurors favored acquittal and five held out for the conviction of Ossian Sweet and Leonard Morse on a charge of manslaughter. See Levine, 183; *Detroit Times* 27 and 28 November 1925; *Detroit Free Press* 27 and 28 November 1925. In the second trial, Henry Sweet was tried alone. Brilliantly defended by Darrow, he was acquitted and all charges against the others were dropped by the prosecuting attorney, Robert M. Toms. See Levine, 185-90; *Detroit News* 21 July 1927; *Detroit Free Press* 22 July 1927.

46. Katzman, *Before the Ghetto*, 207-08.

47. Allan H. Spear, *Black Chicago: The Making of a Negro Ghetto, 1890-1920* (Chicago: University of Chicago Press, 1967); Gilbert Osofsky, "The Enduring Ghetto," *Journal of American History* 55 (1966): 243.

48. Katzman, *Before the Ghetto*, 208.

49. Why did black immigrants, first and second generation, not experience the same patterns of mobility that other groups had experienced? Why the anachronistic or "backward development?" In studying nineteenth century Boston, Pleck identified an anachronistic pattern similar to that in Detroit described by Zunz and Katzman.

On the basis of extensive research, Thernstrom eliminated rural background, educational deficiencies, residential segregation, and female-headed households as good explanations for the anachronistic development, and therefore concluded that the barrier to black economic achievement was racial prejudice.

Others have argued that the change from the convention system of selecting candidates for public office to a primary system eliminated blacks from meaningful participation in the political process. Thus, as a result of reforms and the adoption of the good government charter "blacks were less in the mainstream of American life than they had been in the previous four decades. With politics their last important link with the white community cut of by reform, blacks were left even more isolated" (Katzman 211).

50. Zunz, *Inequality*, 398; Louis Wirth, *The Ghetto* (Chicago: University of Chicago Press, 1928) 283; also I. Krystol, "The Negro Today Is Like the Immigrant Yesterday," *New York Times: Sunday Magazine* 11 September 1966.

51. Zunz, *Inequality*, 398.

52. Zunz, *Inequality*, 398.

53. Richard Thomas, "The Black Urban Experience in Detroit: 1916-1967," in *Blacks and Chicanos in Urban Michigan*, ed. Homer C. Hawkins and Richard W. Thomas (Lansing: Michigan History Division, Michigan Department of State, 1979).

54. Thomas, "The Black Urban Experience," 60-62.

55. U.S. Department of Commerce, "Mortality Statistics: Thirty-First Annual Report, 1930," and Ulysses W. Boykin, *A Handbook on the Detroit Negro* (Detroit: The Minority Study Associates, 1943).

56. Thomas, "The Black Urban Experience in Detroit," 62.

57. Not all blacks in the Detroit area lived in overcrowded tenements or boarding houses. By 1929, there was a small neighborhood on the west side where about 15-20% of the black population lived in their own homes. Nevertheless, boarding was the typical experience, and in 1925 it was found that more than half of 1,000 black families surveyed were taking in boarders (*Pipp's Weekly* 23 November 1929; and Washington, "The Negro in Detroit," vol. 4.).

58. Thomas, "The Black Urban Experience," 62.

59. Ford Motor Company Archive, Lewis's typescript essay, 1954: 13.

60. Ford Motor Company Archive, Accession 62, Box 59.

61. Ford Motor Company Archive, Accession 38, Box 118: "Bradby to Sorensen."

62. Ford Motor Company Archive, Accession 23, Box 3.

63. Ford Motor Company Archive, Accession 62, Box 5.

64. Ford Motor Company Archive, Accession 38, Box 123, "Payroll Department Report on number of Negroes employed at the Rouge plant," February 21, 1940.

65. Olivier Zunz, *Making America Corporate, 1870-1920* (Chicago: University of Chicago Press, 1990) 137.

66. Ford R. Bryan, *Henry's Lieutenants* (Detroit: Wayne State University Press, 1993) 216.

67. Bryan, *Henry's Lieutenants,* 252.

68. Bryan, *Henry's Lieutenants,* 16.

69. Nevins, *Ford,* 523, 518.

70. Zunz, *Making America Corporate,* 135.

71. Zunz, *Making America Corporate,* 134.

72. Zunz, *Making America Corporate,* 136.

73. Quoted in Kanigel, "Frederick Taylor's Apprenticeship," *The Wilson Quarterly* 20.3 (Summer 1996): 50.

6. Ford's Welfare Work: Americanization
and the Molding of the Ford Man

1. Ford Motor Company Archive, Accession 63, Box 1: S.S. Marquis, "Profit Sharing"; John R. Lee, "The So-Called Profit Sharing System in the Ford Plant," *Annals AAPSS* 45 (1916): 299, 308; O.J. Abell, "The Making of Men, Motor Cars, and Profits," *Iron Age* 95 (1915): 37; John A. Fitch, "Ford of Detroit and His Ten Million Dollar Profit Sharing Plan," *Survey* 31 (1915): 545-50.

2. Stephen Meyer III, *The Five Dollar Day: Labor Management and Social Control in the Ford Motor Company, 1908-1921* (Albany: State University of New York Press, 1982) 108.

3. Ford Motor Company Archive, Accession 940.

4. Daniel Nelson, *Managers and Workers: Origins of the New Factory System in the United States, 1880-1920* (Madison: University of Wisconsin Press, 1975) 101. For discussions of the various origins and assumptions about welfare work, see Henry Eilbirt, "The Development of Personnel Management in the United States," *Business History Review* 33 (1959); Don D. Lescohier, "Working Conditions," vol. 3 of John R. Commons, et al., *History of Labor in the United States, 1896-1932* (New York: Macmillan, 1935); Leon P. Alford, "The Status of Industrial Relations," *Mechanical Engineering* 41 (1919); United States Bureau of Labor Statistics, Bulletin 250: 13.

5. There are competing interpretations with regard to the motives of the Ford Motor Company's decision to institute the five-dollar day. Given the setting in which the plan was adopted, the assertion that the plan was in response to a flurry of union activity must be taken seriously. However, such a discussion is well beyond the scope of this study. See also Martha Banta, *Taylored Lives: Narrative Productions in the Age of Taylor, Veblen and Ford* (Chicago: University of Chicago Press, 1993) 26.

6. Charles E. Sorensen, *My Forty Years with Ford* (New York: Norton, 1969) 142. Sorenson's opinion is, as are the opinions of all observers, undoubtedly biased but representative of Ford insiders and sympathizers. James Couzens, who at the time was vice president of the Ford Motor Company, stated in a press interview that he thought the profit-sharing plan was good, and that it might serve as an example for other employers (*New York Times* 6 January 1914). On the other side of the issue, Meyer has suggested, "In the end, Ford paternalism failed, and perhaps, even proved irrelevant." Remembering that the five-dollar day was but a part of a larger effort that included the Americanization campaign, Meyer remarked, "Perhaps the most significant feature of the Ford Americanization program was its failure and eventual termination." Clearly, Meyer's bias is opposite that of Henry Ford, Couzens, Liebold, et al. See Stephen Meyer, "Adapting the Immigrant to the Line: Americanization in the Ford Factory, 1914-1921," *Journal of Social History* 14 (1980).

7. Ford Motor Company Archive, Oral History Section: "Reminiscences of E.G. Liebold," 226.

8. Allen Nevins, *Ford: The Times, the Man, the Company* (New York: Scribner, 1954) 550.

9. The problem of turnover was a major concern at the Crystal Palace as elsewhere in the automotive industry. Henry Eilbirt has noted that around 1910 "a new idea" played an important part in advancing personnel administration. Specifically, in an environment bent on achieving efficiency in production, the computations of Alexander Fischer, et al., revealed theretofore hidden costs of considerable magnitude in labor turnover. "After c.1910, one could scarcely read any subsequent treatment having to do with labor, whether written by friend or critic, executive, physician, psychologist, psychiatrist or any academic student, which omits some mention of turnover as a universal evil to be avoided." Moreover, "Less than a decade had passed before some were concluding that," the key measure of incompetence was the level of turnover (Eilbirt, "Development of Personnel Management," 356); Magnus W. Alexander, "Hiring and Firing," *Annals AAPSS* 65 (1919); Boyd Fisher, "Methods of Reducing the Labor Turnover," *Annals* May 1919.

10. Ford Motor Company Archive, Accession 940, Box 17: "Instructions to Investigators."

11. Olivier Zunz, *The Changing Face of Inequality: Urbanization, Industrial Development, and Immigration in Detroit, 1880-1920* (Chicago: University of Chicago Press, 1982) 311.

12. Lee, "Profit Sharing System," 302-09.

13. Lee, "Profit Sharing System," 302-09.

14. Lee, "Profit Sharing System," 300; Meyer, *Five Dollar Day*, 104.

15. Oliver J. Abell, "The Ford Plan for Employees," *Iron Age* 29 January 1914; Meyer, *Five Dollar Day*, 127; Zunz, *Making America Corporate*, 134, and note 27, 240-41.

16. Ford Motor Company Archive, Accession 62, Box 19: Letters from Lacking and Helfman, and Lacking and Hanlon to Leibold, dated July 3, 1915.

17. Both Stephen Meyer and Allen Nevins have written extraordinarily incisive chapter-length discussions on the Sociological Department. Hence, this study includes only the details essential to elucidation of questions raised here.

18. Olivier Zunz, *Making America Corporate*, 1870-1920 (Chicago: University of Chicago Press, 1990) 135.

19. Ford Motor Company Archive, Accession 940, Box 17: "Instructions to Investigators."

20. The Crystal Palace had about 250 women workers at the time. A vocal outcry from feminist leaders such as Helen Keller and Anna Howard Shaw apparently persuaded the Ford Motor Company to include women in profit-sharing (Meyer, *Five Dollar Day*).

21. Ford Motor Company Archive, Accession 62, Box 58: "Report of Sociological Department," October 12, 1914.

22. Meyer, *Five Dollar Day*, 123; Boris Emmet, "Profit Sharing in the United States," *Bulletin of the Bureau of Labor Statistics* 208 (1916): 106; Ford Motor Company, "Helpful Hints," 13.

23. Ford Motor Company Archive, Accession 293, Box 1: "Profit Sharing."

24. Harold C. Hill, "The Americanization Movement," *The American Journal of Sociology* 24.6 (1919): 613.

25. David M. Kennedy, *Over Here: World War and American Society* (New York: Oxford University Press, 1980) 63.

26. Kennedy, *Over Here: World War and American Society*, 63.

27. John Higham, *Strangers in the Land: Patterns of American Nativism, 1860-1925* (New York: Atheneum, 1963) 263; cited in Kennedy, *Over Here*, 64.

28. Gerd Korman, *Industrialization: Immigrants and Americanizers* (Madison State Historical Society of Wisconsin, 1967) 144; see also, Korman's "Americanization at The Factory Gate," *Industrial and Labor Relations Review* 18 (April 1965).

29. Korman, *Industrialization: Immigrants and Americanizers*, 144; also Nelson, *Managers and Workers*.

30. *Ford Times*, 2 December 1908: 1; Meyer, *Five Dollar Day*, 68-69.

31. Meyer, *Five Dollar Day*, 68; Zunz, *Changing Face of Inequality*, 313; Nelson, *Managers and Workers*, 144-45.

32. Hill, "The Americanization Movement," 633.

33. Nelson, *Managers and Workers*, 144-45.

34. *Articles of Association of the Americanization Committee of Detroit*, Article 1, section 2 (1925)/*ACD Papers*: 3.

35. Higham, *Strangers in the Land*, 243; Hill, "The Americanization movement," 617; Zunz, *Changing Face of Inequality*, 313.

36. Zunz, *Changing Face of Inequality*, 313; Levine, *Internal Combustion*, 28.

37. "Members of the Education Committee of the Detroit Board of Commerce to Corporation Executives," May 1915, ACD Papers; also Membership lists and communications in A.J. Tuttle AMC Papers, MHC; Zunz, *Changing Face of Inequality*, 314; Levine, *Internal Combustion*, 27-28.

38. Levine, *Internal Combustion*, 28.

39. Ford Motor Company Archive, Accession 683: "Letter to Omaha, January 29, 1914; cited in Meyer, *Five Dollar Day*, 150-51.

40. Gregory Mason, "Americans First: How the People of Detroit Are Making Americans of Foreigners in their City," *Outlook* 114 (27 September 1915): 200; S.S. Marquis, "The Ford Idea in Education," in National Education Association, *Addresses and Proceedings*, 1916, vol. 64 (1916): 911-16 passim; Clinton C. DeWitt, "Industrial Teachers," in United States Bureau of Education, *Proceedings Americanization Conference* (Washington, D.C., 1919): 116; also Ester Evrett Lape, "The English First Movement in Detroit," *Immigration in America Review* 1 (September 1915): 46-50; Meyer, *Five Dollar Day*, 161.

41. Ford Motor Company Archive, Accession 940, "Preliminary Report of Work Done Teaching the English Language to Employees of the Ford Motor Company at Stevens School, Highland Park, Michigan, June 12, 1914; Peter Roberts, *English For Coming Americans* (New York: YMCA Press, 1909) 20-23; Meyer, *Five Dollar Day*, 157.

42. S.S. Marquis, "The Ford Idea in Education," 911-16, passim; Meyer, *Five Dollar Day*, 156.

43. Ford Motor Company Archive, Accession 1, Box 21: "Report on Ford Language School, March 1916."

44. Ford Motor Company Archive, Accession 572, Box 27; Ford Motor Company Archive, Accession 62, Box 59.

45. Ford Motor Company Archive, Accession 572, Box 31.

46. Horace L. Arnold and Fay L. Faurote, *Ford Methods and Ford Shops* (New York: Engineering Magazine Company, 1916) 330.

47. Joel John Lowery, "Labor Relations in the Automobile Industry During the Nineteen Twenties," Master's Thesis, Michigan State University, 1958.

48. Ford Motor Company Archive, Oral History Section: "The Reminiscences of William P. Baxter," 15.

49. Michigan Department of Labor, "Record of Accidents Given by Counties," *Thirty-second Annual Report* (1915).

50. Ford Motor Company Archive, Accession 62, Box 59.

51. U.S. Department of Labor. Children's Bureau, *Minors in Automobile and Metal-Manufacturing Industries in Michigan*, Bureau Publication No. 126, 1923. 57-59.

52. U.S. Department of Labor, *Minors in Automobile Industries*, 57-59.

53. Martha Banta, *Taylored Lives: Narrative Productions in the Age of Taylor, Veblen, and Ford* (Chicago: University of Chicago Press, 1993) 26.

54. Quoted in Fisher, "How to Reduce Labor Turnover," 33.

7. Ford Men Living In

1. Ida M. Tarbell, *All in the Day's Work: An Autobiography* (New York: Macmillan, 1939) 289-90.

2. Ford Motor Company Archive, Accession 293, Box 1: "Profit Sharing"; also cited in Stephen Meyer, III, *The Five Dollar Day: Labor Management and Social Control in the Ford Motor Company, 1908-1921* (Albany: State University of New York Press, 1991) 133.

3. John Modell and Tamara K. Hareven "Urbanization and the Malleable Household: An Examination of Boarding and Lodging in American Families," *The American Family in Social and Historical Perspective*, ed. Michael Gordon (New York: St. Martin's, 1978) 52.

4. Modell and Hareven, "Boarding and Lodging," 59.

5. Katherine Hill, Librarian-Curator at McGregor Library-Museum, interview by author, October 1986.

6. *Highland Parker* 2 January 1927.

7. Modell and Hareven, "Boarding and Lodging," 51.

8. Robert W. De Forest and Lawrence Veiller, *The Tenement House Problem*, vol. 1 (New York: Macmillan, 1903) 60.

9. De Forest and Veiller, *Tenement House Problem*, 60-61.

10. *Detroit Saturday Night* 7.21 (19 July 1913).

11. Ford Motor Company Archive, Accession 62, Box 28: "Outline of Suggestions for Housing of Employees of Henry Ford at Ford Tractor Plants and the River Rouge."

12. Boris Emmett, "Profit Sharing in the United States," *Bulletin of the Bureau of Labor Statistics* (1916): 99-100.

13. Emmet, "Profit Sharing," 99-100.

14. Ford Motor Company Archive, Accession 940, Box 17: "Human Interest Story Number One."

15. Ford Motor Company Archive, Accession 940, Box 17: "Human Interest Story Number Nine," reported by F. Andrews.

16. Harry Franklin Porter, "Giving the Men a Share: What It's Doing for Ford," *System* 31 (March 1917): 267.

17. Emmet, "Profit Sharing," 99-100.

18. Ford Motor Company Archive, Accession 62, Box 59: "Social Statistics of the Home Plant as of January 12, 1916."

19. Ford Motor Company Archive, Accession 293, Box 11: "S.S. Marquis."

20. Allan Nevins and Frank Ernest Hill, *Ford: The Times* 1954.

21. Ford Motor Company Archive, Accession 940, Box 17: A.E. Gruenberg, "Progress among Foreigners Since Proclamation of Profit Sharing Plan," June 3, 1916.

22. Ford Motor Company Archive, Accession 940, Box 17: "The Board of Health," n.d.

23. Ford Motor Company Archive, Accession 940, Box 17; "S.S. Marquis Papers/Frank Hill Papers."

24. Downriver Genealogical Society Census Holdings (DGS) 1850-1910, Roll 678.

25. U.S. Department of Commerce, Bureau of the Census. *Abstract of the Fourteenth Census of the United Stated: 1920*; also *Special Census of the Population of Highland Park, Michigan, November 15, 1916*.

26. Ford Motor Company, "Helpful Hints," 1915: 13.

27. DGS.

28. DGS

29. DGS.

30. Table 4.2 suggests a considerably lower average of about 25-38.

31. According to the Ford Motor Company, in 1917 the native-born American workers had an average of 1.27 children while Poles (and presumably other ethnics) had about 2.3 (Ford Motor Company Archive, Accession 940, Box 16).

32. There is considerable evidence that the income earned by wives caring for boarders was nealy as important, and often more important, than the incomes earned as wages in jobs such as those in the Crystal Palace. See, for example, Elizabeth H. Pleck's article, "A Mother's Wages: Income Earning Among Married and Black Women, 1896-1911," *A Heritage of Her Own*, ed. Nancy F. Cott and Elizabeth H. Pleck (New York: Simon and Schuster, 1979). Although this article does not focus on the Detroit area, it is nevertheless instructive.

33. *The Ford Times* 15 January 1923 reported that 11,500 cars were driven to work at Ford plants (Ford Motor Company Archive, Accession 940, Box 16).

34. This (perhaps overly generalized) profile of the "average Ford man" is based on observations reported in Chen-Nan Li, "A Summer in the Ford Works," *Personnel Journal* 7 (June 1928): 18-32.

35. Ford Motor Company Archive, Accession 1, Box 126. Fair Lane Papers: "Wages and Hours Program of Anniversary Dinner, January 12, 1915." This lyric was apparently sung to the tune of "Tom Dooley."

36. Ford Motor Company Archive, Accession 572, Box 14: "James Couzens to E.G. Liebold, November 1929."

Conclusion

1. Allan Nevins and Frank Ernest Hill, *Ford: Expansion and Challenge, 1915-1933* (New York: Scribner, 1957) 204.

2. Nevins, *Ford: Expansion*, 257.

3. Lewis, "Ford and Kahn," *Michigan History* 64.5 (1980): 22-23.

4. Nevins, *Ford: Expansion*, 295.

5. Nevins, *Ford: Expansion*, 294.

6. Nevins, *Ford*, 540 cites David L. Lewis, "History of Negro Employment in Detroit Area Plants of the Ford Motor Company 1914-1941," a University of Michigan typescript essay (1954); Ford Motor Company Archive; Willis Ward, "Reminiscences"; Detroit Bureau of Government Research, *The Negro in Detroit*, prepared for the Mayor's Inter-racial Committee, 1926; Herbert R. Northrup, *Organized Labor and the Negro* (New York: Harper, 1944).

7. Nevins, *Ford*, 539.

8. Nevins, *Ford*, 539-40.

9. Olivier Zunz, *The Changing Face of Inequality: Urbanization Industrial Development and Immigration in Detroit, 1880-1920* (Chicago: University of Chicago Press, 1982) 396-97.

10. Nora Faires, "Assembling The History of Detroit," *Michigan Quarterly Review* September 1985; Katzman, *Before the Ghetto: Black Detroit in the Nineteenth Century* (Chicago: University of Illinois Press, 1973).

11. See Appendix B.

12. James Flink, "The Car Culture Revisited: Some Comments on the Recent Historiography of Automotive History," *Michigan Quarterly Review* 4 (Fall 1980 and Winter 1981): 772-81.

13. Ellen Hathaway, *History of Highland Park* (Highland Park, Michigan: Highland Park Board of Education, 1957).

14. U.S. Department of Commerce, *Special Census of Highland Park Michigan, 1915*, emphatically makes this point.

15. The Model T assembly line had been shut down in May 1927, and by 1935 the total number of workers in the Crystal Palace had been reduced to 2,488, of whom 20 were black; in 1940, 18 remained. Regarding the number of black workers in the Crystal Palace, see Ford Motor Company Archive, Accession 23, Box 3; Accession 62, Box 5; and

Accession 38, Box 123, "Payroll Department Report on number of Negroes employed at the Rouge plant," February 21, 1940.

16. Highly placed Ford Motor Company officials often spoke of the significance of improving the quality of life of Ford workers. See, for example, Ford Motor Company Archive, Accession 683: "Letter to Omaha," January 29, 1914.

17. See "Highland Park," in tables 3.3, 3.4 and 3.9 in Joe T. Darden, et al., *Race and Uneven Development* (Philadelphia: Temple University Press, 1987).

Appendix B

1. J. Dennis Willigan, and Katherine A. Lynch, *Sources and Methods of Historical Demography* (New York: Academic Press, 1982).

2. The posthumous publication of Petty's Political Arithmetick (1690) marked a watershed in the methods employed in "social research."

3. Kenneth E. Hornback and Joel Guttman, *Studies in Environment, Vol. 2: Quality of Life* (Washington, D.C.: Government Printing Office, 1973); Ben-Chieh Liv, "Quality of Life: Concept, Measure and Results," *The American Journal of Economics and Sociology* 34.1 (1975); David A. Larson and Walton T. Wilford, "The Physical Quality Life: A Useful Social Indicator?" *World Development*, vol. 7 (1979).

4. Margaret Mead, et al., "Man in Space: A Tool and Program for the Study of Social Change," *Annals of New York Academy of Science* 72.4 (10 April 1958): 165-214.

5. Daniel Bell, "The Adequacy of Our Concepts," *A Great Society*, ed. Bertram M. Gross (New York: Basic Books, 1966) 152.

6. Bertram M. Gross, *The State of the Nation: Social Systems Accounting* (London: Tavistok, 1966); Raymond A. Bauer, *Social Indicators* (Cambridge, Massachusetts: MIT Press, 1966).

7. EPA, "Quality of Life," 7.

8. U.S. Department of Health, Education and Welfare, *Toward a Social Report* (Washington, D.C.: Government Printing Office, 1969).

9. HEW, Social Report.

10. U.S. Environmental Protection Agency, "Quality of Life Studies in Environment," vol. 2, by Kenneth E. Hornback, et al. (Washington, D.C.: Government Printing Office, 1973), 15.

11. EPA, "Quality of Life," 71.

12. EPA, "Quality of Life," 75.

13. Although there is a lack of consensus in many areas, Lui's review of several empirical studies (including *Lifetime Magazine* 1972; Wilson, 1967; and *The Geography of Social Well-Being in the U.S.*, by Smith,

1973) found that while the studies were based on different definitions of the QOL, employed different criteria for variable selection, and used different years, there was a very high correlation in state rankings of the QOL barometer. See Ben-Chieh Lui, "Quality of Life: Concept and Measure, and Results," *The American Journal of Economics and Sociology* 34.1 (1975).

Further evidence of convergence of a sort, may be inferred from David Larson and Walton Wilford's assessment of the PQLI. The Overseas Development Council (ODC) provides a measurement called the Physical Quality of Life Index (PQLI) that combines infant mortality, life expectancy, and literacy into a single index. The results of statistical tests showed that any one of the three PQLI variables would serve as well alone as the composite index does in ranking life quality; hence, the PQLI is not a major new indicator of inter-country human welfare. (See David A. Larson and Walton T. Wilford, "The Physical Quality of Life Index: A Useful Social Indicator?" *World Development*, vol. 7, 1979.)

14. H.J. Dyos, "Some Historical Reflections on the Quality of Life," *The Quality of Urban Life*, ed. Henry J. Schmandt and Varner Bloomberg, Jr. (Beverly Hills, California: Sage Publications, 1969) 38.

Selected Bibliography

Books and Pamphlets

Alston, Christopher C. *Henry Ford and the Negro People*. Washington: National Negro Congress; Detroit: Michigan Negro Congress, 1941.

Arnold, Horace Lucien, and Fay Leone. Faurote. *Ford Methods and the Ford Shops*. 1915; reprinted, New York: Arno, 1972.

Babson, Steve. *Working Detroit: The Making of a Union Town*. New York: Adama Books, 1984.

Banta, Martha. *Taylored Lives: Narrative Productions in the Age of Taylor, Veblen and Ford*. Chicago: University of Chicago Press, 1993.

Bluestone, Barry, and Bennett Harrison. *The Deindustrializaton of America: Plant Closings, Community Abandonment, and the Dismantlng of Basic Industry*. New York: Basic Books, 1982.

Bolkosky, Sidney. *Harmony and Dissonance: Voices of Jewish Identity in Detroit, 1914-1967*. Detroit: Wayne State University Press, 1991.

Brandes, Stuart D. *American Welfare Capitalism, 1880-1940*. Chicago: University of Chicago Press, 1976.

Braverman, Harry. *Labor and Monopoly Capital: The Degradation of Work in the Twentieth Century*. New York: Monthly Review Press, 1974.

Bryan, Ford R. *Henry's Lieutenants*. Detroit: Wayne State University Press, 1993.

Bucci, Federico. *Albert Kahn: Architect of Ford*. New York: Princeton Architectural Press, 1993.

Burton, Clarence M., ed. *The City of Detroit, Michigan*. 5 vols. Chicago: Clarke, 1922.

——, and M. Agnes, eds. *History of Wayne County and Detroit, Michigan*. Chicago: Clarke, 1930.

Campbell, Angus, and Philip E. Converse. *The Human Meaning of Social Change*. New York: Russell Sage Foundation, 1972.

Catlin, George G. *The Story of Detroit*. Detroit: Detroit News, 1923. This is a collection of newspaper articles originally published in the *News* during 1923.

Chandler, Alfred D. *The Visible Hand: The Managerial Revolution in American Business*. Cambridge: Belknap Press Harvard University, 1977.

Clymer, Floyd. *Henry's Wonderful Model T 1908-1927*. New York: Bonanza Books, 1945.

Cooper, Gail. "Frederick Winslow Taylor and Scientific Management." *Technology in America*. Ed. Carroll W. Pursell. Cambridge: MIT Press, 1990. 161-76.

Darden, Joe T. et al. *Detroit: Race and Uneven Development*. Philadelphia: Temple University Press, 1987.

De Forest, Robert W., and Lawrence Veiller, eds. *The Tenement House Problem, Including the Report of the New York State Tenement House Commission of 1900*. 2 vols. New York: Macmillan, 1903.

Dunn, Robert W. *Labor and Automobiles*. New York: International Publishers, 1929.

Feinstein, Otto. "Why Ethnicity?" *Immigrants and Migrants: The Detroit Ethnic Experience*. Ed. David W. Hartman. Detroit: New University Thought, 1974. 2-9.

Flink, James. *America Adopts the Automobile, 1895-1910* Cambridge, Mass.: MIT Press, 1970.

——. "Henry Ford and the Triumph of the Automobile." *Technology in America*. Ed. Carroll W. Pursell. Cambridge: MIT Press, 1990. 177-89.

Ford, Henry. *My Life and Work*. Garden City: Doubleday, 1922.

Ford Motor Company. *Bonus, Investment, and Profit Sharing Plan: An Extension to Profit Sharing*. Highland Park, Mich.: Ford Motor Company, 1919.

——. *Facts from Ford*. Highland Park, Mich.: Ford Motor Company, 1920.

——. *The Ford Idea in Education*. Detroit: Ford Motor Company, 1917.

——. *Helpful Hints and Advice to Employees to Help Them Grasp the Opportunities Which Are Presented to Them by the Ford Profit Sharing Plan*. Detroit: Ford Motor Company, 1915.

Fragnoli, Raymond R. *The Transformation of Reform: Progressivism in Detroit—and After, 1912-1933*. New York: Garland, 1982.

Gelderman, Carol W. *Henry Ford: The Wayward Capitalist*. New York: Dial Press, 1981.

Glazer, Sidney. *Detroit: A Study in Urban Development*. New York: Bookman, 1965.

Greenstone, David. *A Report on the Politics of Detroit*. Cambridge: Joint Center for Urban Studies of Massachusetts Institute of Technology and Harvard University, 1961.

Hatch, Nathan O., ed. *The Professions in American History*. Notre Dame: University of Notre Dame Press, 1988.

Hathaway, Ellen. *History of Highland Park*. Highland Park, Mich: Highland Park Board of Education, 1957.

Haynes, George E. *Negro Newcomers in Detroit, Michigan: A Challenge to Christian Statesmanship, A Preliminary Survey*. 1918; reprint, New York: Arno Press and The New York Times, 1969.

Hecock, Donald S. *Detroit Voters and Recent Elections*. Detroit: Detroit Bureau of Governmental Research, 1938.

Hendrickson, Wilma Wood, ed. *Detroit Perspectives: Crossroads and Turning Points*. Detroit: Wayne State University Press, 1991.

Henri, Florette. *Black Migration: Movement North, 1900-1920*. Garden City: Anchor Press-Doubleday, 1975.

Higham, John. *Strangers in the Land: Patterns of American Nativism*. New York: Atheneum, 1963.

Hoxie, Robert F. *Scientific Management and Labor*. New York: Appleton, 1916.

Jones, Franklin D. *Jig and Fixture Design*. New York: Industrial Press, 1920.

Katzman, David M. *Before the Ghetto: Black Detroit in the Nineteenth Century*. Chicago: University of Illinois Press, 1973.

Kellog, Paul U. "Ford Motor Company's Changeover from the Model T." *Detroit Perspectives: Cross Roads and Turning Points*. Ed. Wilma Wood Henrickson. Detroit: Wayne State University Press, 1990. 351-61.

Kelly, Alfred H., Winfred A. Harbison, and Herman Belz. *The American Constitution*. 6th ed. New York: Norton, 1968.

Kennedy, David M. *Over Here: The First World War and American Society*. New York: Oxford University Press, 1980.

Korman, Gerd. *Industrialization, Immigrants and Americanizers*. Madison: State Historical Society of Wisconsin, 1967.

Koscielski, Regina. "Portrait of a Polish-American." *Immigrants and Migrants: The Detroit Ethnic Experience*. Ed. David W. Hartman. Detroit: New University Thought, 1974. 114-18.

Lacey, Robert. *Ford: the Men and the Machine*. Boston: Little, Brown, 1986.

Lescohier, Don. "Working Conditions." *History of Labor in the United States, 1896-1932*. 3 vols. Ed. John R. Commons. New York: Macmillan, 1935.

Levine, David Allan. *Internal Combustion: The Races in Detroit, 1915-1926*. Westport: Greenwood Press, 1976.

Levine, Leo. *Ford: The Dust and the Glory, A Racing History*. New York: Macmillan, 1968.

Lieberson, Stanley. *A Piece of the Pie: Black and White Immigrants Since 1880*. Los Angeles: University of California Press, 1980.

Livesay, Harold C. "The Profession of Management in the United States." *The Professions in American History*. Ed. Nathan O. Hatch. Notre Dame: University of Notre Dame Press, 1988. 199-220.

May, George S. *A Most Unique Machine: The Michigan Origins of the American Automobile Industry*. Grand Rapids, Mich: Eerdman's, 1975.

Marquis, Samuel S. *Henry Ford: An Interpretation.* Boston: Little Brown, 1923.

McCalley, Bruce W. *Model T Ford: The Car That Changed the World.* Iola, Wisc.: Krause, 1994.

Meyer, Stephen, III. *The Five Dollar Day: Labor Management and Social Control in the Ford Motor Company, 1908-1921.* Albany: State University of New York Press, 1981.

Modell, John, and Tamara K. Hareven, "Urbanization and the Malleable Household: An Examination of Boarding and Lodging in American Families" *The American Family in Social and Historical Perspective.* Ed. Michael Gordon. New York: St. Martin's, 1978. 51-68.

Montgomery, David. *Worker's Control in America: Studies in the History of Work, Technology, and Labor Struggles.* Cambridge: Cambridge University Press, 1979.

Nelson, Daniel. *Managers and Workers: Origins of the Factory System in the United States. 2nd ed.* Madison, Wisc.: University of Wisconsin Press, 1995.

Nevins, Allan. *Ford: Decline and Rebirth, 1933-1962.* New York: Scribner, 1963.

——. *Ford: The Times, the Man, the Company.* New York: Scribner, 1954.

——, and Frank Ernest Hill. *Ford: Expansion and Challenge, 1915-1933.* New York: Scribner, 1957.

Northrup, Herbert R. *The Negro in the Automobile Industry.* Philadelphia: Wharton School of Finance and Commerce, University of Pennsylvania Press, 1968.

Norwood, Edwin. *Ford Men and Methods.* Garden City: Doubleday, 1922.

Page, Victor W. *Ford Owner's Handbook of Repair & Maintenance: Models T and A.* Los Angeles: Clymer, 1953.

Pleck, Elizabeth H. *Black Migration and Poverty: Boston, 1865-1900.* New York: Academic Press, 1979.

——. "A Mother's Wages: Income Earning Among Black Women, 1896-1911." *A Heritage of Her Own.* Ed. Nancy F. Cott and Elizabeth H. Pleck. New York: Simon and Schuster, 1979.

Pred, Allan R. *The Spacial Dynamics of U.S. Urban-Industrial Growth, 1800-1914.* Cambridge: MIT Press, 1966.

Pursell, Carroll W., ed. *Technology in America: A History of Individuals and Ideas.* Cambridge: MIT Press, 1990.

Reitell, Charles. *How to be a Good Foreman.* New York: Ronald Press, c. 1937.

——. *Machinery and Its Benefits to Labor in the Crude Iron and Steel Industries.* Menasha, Wisc.: Banta, 1917.

——. *Training Workers and Supervisors*. New York: Ronald Press, 1941.

Roberts, Peter. *English for Coming Americans*. New York: YMCA Press,1909.

Rothschild, Emma. *Paradise Lost: The Decline of the Auto-Industrial Age*. New York: Random House, 1973.

Rossiter, William S. *Increase of Population in the United States, 1910-1920*. Washington, D.C.: Government Printing Office, 1922.

Schmandt, Henry J., and Varner Bloomberg, Jr. *The Quality of Urban Life*. Beverly Hills, Calif.: Sage Publications, 1969.

Schneider, John C. *Detroit and the Problem of Order, 1830-1880*. Lincoln: University of Nebraska Press, 1980.

Schofield, R.S. "Sampling In Historical Research." *Nineteenth Century Society*. Ed. E.A. Wrigley. Cambridge: Cambridge University Press, 1972.

Schwartz, Jonathan. "Henry Ford's Melting Pot." *Immigrants and Migrants: The Detroit Ethnic Experience*. Ed. David W. Hartman. Detroit: New University Thought, 1974. 252-59.

Scott, Emmet J. *Negro Migration During the War*. New York: Oxford University Press, 1920.

Sengstock, Mary G. "The Ethnic Grosse Pointe." *Immigrants and Migrants: The Detroit Ethnic Experience*. Ed. David W. Hartman. Detroit: New University Thought, 1974. 339-44.

Sheldon, Eleanor B., and Wilbert E. Moore. *Indicators of Social Change: Concepts and Measurements*. New York: Russell Sage Foundation, 1968.

Sinclair, Upton. *The Flivver King: A Story of Ford America*. Station A, Pasadena, Calif.: United Auto Workers, 1937.

Smith, D.M. *The Geography of Social Well-Being in the U.S.* New York: McGraw-Hill, 1973.

Sorensen, Charles E. *My Forty Years with Ford*. New York: Norton, 1956.

Stephanides, Marios. "Detroit's Greek Community." *Immigrants and Migrants: The Detroit Ethnic Experience*. Ed. David W. Hartman. Detroit: New University Thought, 1974. 326-37.

Sward, Keith. *The Legend of Henry Ford*. New York: Russell and Russell, 1948.

Tarbell, Ida M. *All in the Day's Work: An Autobiography*. New York: Macmillan, 1939.

Taylor, Frederick Winslow. *Scientific Management*. New York: Harper, 1947.

Taylor, Paul. *Prosperity in Detroit*. Highland Park, Mich: Paul Taylor, 1920.

Thernstrom, Stephan. *The Other Bostonians: Poverty and Progress in the American Metropolis, 1880-1970*. Cambridge: Harvard University Press, 1973.

———. *Poverty and Progress: Social Mobility in a Nineteenth-Century City*. Cambridge: Harvard University Press, 1964.

Thomas, Richard W. "The Black Urban Experience in Detroit, 1916-1967." *Blacks and Chicanos in Urban Michigan*. Ed. Homer C. Hawkins and Richard Thomas. Lansing, Mich.: Michigan History Division, Michigan Department of State, 1979.

Thompson, E.P. *The Making of the English Working Class*. New York: Vintage, 1963.

Van Doren Stern, Philip. *Tin Lizzie*. New York: Simon and Schuster, 1955.

Warner, Sam Bass, and Sylvia Fleisch. *Measurement for Social History*. Beverly Hills, Calif.: Sage Press, 1977.

Washington, Forrester B. *The Negro in Detroit: A Survey of Conditions of a Negro Group in a Northern Industrial Center during the War Prosperity Period*. Detroit: Research Bureau, Associated Charities of Detroit, 1920.

Weibe, Robert H. *The Search for Order, 1877-1920*. New York: Hill and Wang, 1967.

Wik, Reynold M. *Henry Ford and Grass-Roots America*. Ann Arbor, Mich.: University of Michigan Press, 1972.

Willigan, J. Dennis, and Katherine A. Lynch. *Sources and Methods of Historical Demography*. New York: Academic Press, 1982.

Wilson, John Oliver. *Quality of Life in the United States: An Excursion into the New Frontier of Socio-Economic Indicators*. Kansas City: Midwest Research Institute, 1967 and 1979.

Writer's Program of the Work Projects Administration in Michigan. *Michigan: A Guide to the Wolverine State*. New York: Oxford University Press, 1941.

Zunz, Olivier. *The Changing Face of Inequality: Urbanization, Industrial Development, and Immigration in Detroit, 1880-1920*. Chicago: University of Chicago Press, 1982.

———. *Making America Corporate, 1870-1920*. Chicago: University of Chicago Press, 1990.

Periodicals

Abell, Oliver J. "The Ford Plan for Employees' Betterment." *Iron Age* 93 (29 January 1914): 306-09.

———. "Labor Classified on a Skill-Wages Basis." *Iron Age* 93 (1 January 1914): 48-51.

———. "Making the Ford Motor Car." *Iron Age* 89 (6 June 1912): 1383; 90 (13 June 1912): 1454-60.

——. "The Making of Men, Motor Cars and Profits." *Iron Age* 95 (7 January 1915): 33-41.

Ackerson, Robert C. "Historiography: Some Milestones of Automotive Literature." *Michigan Quarterly Review* 4 (Fall 1980); 1 (Winter 1981): 761-71.

Alexander, Magnus W. "Hiring and Firing: Its Economic Wastes and How to Avoid It." *Annals* 65 (May 1916): 128-44.

Alford, Leon P. "The Status of Industrial Relations." *Industrial Management* 58 (July 1919): 61-66.

Arnold, Horace L. "Ford Methods and Ford Shops." *Engineering Magazine.* A series of articles from April 1914 to February 1915.

Bailer, Lloyd H. "The Negro Automobile Worker." *Journal of Political Economy* 51 (October 1943): 415-28.

Blankenbaker, Joe. "Ford, Henry." Rev. of *Ford: The Dust and the Glory*, by Leo Levine. *Biographical Dictionary of American Sports* (1988): 9-10.

Bloomberg, Susan E., Frank Fox, et al. "A Census Probe into Nineteenth Century Family History: Southern Michigan 1850-1880." *Journal of Social History* 5 (Fall 1971): 27-45.

Bornholt, Oscar C. "Placing Machines for Sequences and Use." *Iron Age* 92 (4 December 1913): 1276-77.

Brody, David. "The Old Labor History and the New: In Search of an American Working Class." *Labor History* 20 (Winter 1979): 109-26.

Bundy, George. "Work of The Employment Department of the Ford Motor Company." *Bulletin of the Bureau of Labor Statistics* 196 (1916): 63-67.

Colvin, Fred. "Continuous Pouring in the Ford Foundry." *American Machinist* 39 (1913): 910-12.

——. "Ford Camshaft Machining Methods." *American Machinist* 39 (3 July 1913): 9-12.

——. "Ford Production Methods." *American Machinist* 3 May and 18 September 1913. A series of fourteen articles.

——. "Machining the Ford Cylinders-I." *American Machinist* 38 (22 May 1913): 841-46.

——. "Methods Employed in Making the Ford Magneto." *American Machinist* 39 (21 August 1913): 311-16.

Davis, Kingsley, and Pietronellavan den Oever. "Demographic Foundations of New Sex Roles." *Population Development Review* 8.3 (1982): 495-511.

De Matteo, Arthur E. "Organized Labor Versus the Mayor: The Detroit Federation of Labor and the Revised City Charter of 1914." *Michigan Historical Review* 21.2 (1995): 38-63.

Donald, Henderson H. "The Negro Migration of 1916-1918." *Journal of Negro History* 6 (October 1921): 383-498.

DuBois, W.E.B. "The Migration of Negroes." *The Crisis* 14.2 (1917): 63-66.

Duncan, Otis Dudley. "Toward Social Reporting: Next Steps." *Social Science Frontiers*. New York: Russell Sage Foundation, 1969.

Eilbirt, Henry. "The Development of Personnel Management in the United States." *Business History Review* 33 (1959): 345-64.

Emmet, Boris. "Profit Sharing in the United States." *Bulletin of the Bureau of Labor Statistics*, 1916.

Faires, Nora. "Assembling the History of Detroit." *Michigan Quarterly Review* 25.2 (1986): 468-78.

Faurote, Fay L. "Ford Methods and Ford Shops." *Engineering Magazine* 48 (March 1915): 859-76.

Fisher, Boyd. "Methods of Reducing Labor Turnover." 65 *Annals* (May 1916): 144-54.

Fitch, John A. "Ford of Detroit and His Ten Million Dollar Profit Sharing Plan." *Survey* 31 (1915): 545-50.

Flink, James. "The Car Culture Revisited: Some Comments on the Recent Historiography of Automotive History." *Michigan Quarterly* 4 (Fall 1980–Winter 1981): 772-81.

Foster, Mark S. "The Model T, The Hard Sell, and Los Angeles Urban Growth: The Decentralization of Los Angeles During the 1920s." *Pacific Historical Review* 44.4 (November 1975): 459-84.

Glazer, Sidney. "The Michigan Labor Movement." *Michigan History* 29 (January-March 1945): 73-83.

Gutman, Herbert. "Work, Culture, and Society in Industrial America." *American Historical Review* 78 (July1973): 531-87.

Hill, Howard C. "The Americanization Movement." *American Journal of Sociology* 24 (May 1919): 609-42.

Hunt, Chester L. "Female Occupational Roles and Urban Sex Ratios in the United States, Japan and The Philippines." *Social Forces* 43 (March 1965): 407-17.

Kalleberg, Arne, and Larry Griffin. "Class, Occupation, and Inequality in Job Rewards." *American Journal of Sociology* 85.4 (1980): 731-68.

Kanigel, Robert. "Frederick Taylor's Apprenticeship." *The Wilson Quarterly* 20.3 (Summer 1996): 44-51.

Laird, Raymond H. "I Worked for Mr. Ford." *Dearborn Historian* 10.1 (1970): 2-18.

Larson, David A., and Walton T. Wilfred. "The Physical Quality of Life Index: A Useful Social Indicator." *World Development* 7 (1979): 581-84.

Lee, Everett S. "A Theory of Migration." *Demography* 2.1 (1966): 47-58.

Lee, John R. "The So-Called Profit Sharing System in The Ford Plant." *Annals of the American Academy of Political and Social Science* 65 (May 1916): 297-310.

Levin, Samuel M. "The End of Ford Profit Sharing." *Personnel Journal* 6 (October 1927): 161-70.

——. "Ford Profit Sharing 1914-1920-I: The Growth of the Plan." *Personnel Journal* 6 (August 1927): 75-86.

Lewis, David. "Ford and Kahn." *Michigan History* 64.5 (1980): 17-28.

Li, Chen-Nan. "A Summer in The Ford Works." *Personnel Journal* 7 (June 1928): 118-32.

Lovett, William P. "Detroit and Its New Charter." *National Municipal Review* 10 (March 1921):149-51.

Lui, Ben-Chieh. "Quality of Life: Concept, Measure and Results." *American Journal of Economics and Sociology* 34.1 (1975): 1-13.

Madison, Charles. "My Seven Years of Automotive Servitude." *Michigan Quarterly* 4 (Fall 1980–Winter 1981): 445-58.

Mandel, Bernard. "Samuel Gompers and the Negro Workers, 1886-1914." *Journal of Negro History* 40 (1955): 34-60.

Marglin, Stephen A. "What Do Bosses Do?: Origins and Functions of Hierarchy in Capitalist Production." *Review of Radical Political Economy* 6 (Summer 1974): 60-112.

Martin, I.T. "The Melting Pot at Ford's: Conditions of Employees Under the New Profit Sharing System." *Official Journal* (CWAWU) 4 (August 1915): 5-8.

Mead, J.E. "Rehabilitating Cripples at the Ford Plant." *Iron Age* 102 (26 September 1918): 739-42.

Meyer, Stephen. "Adapting the Immigrant to the Line: Americanization in the Ford Factory, 1914-1921." *Journal of Social History* (Fall 1980): 67-82.

Milbrath, Lester W. "A Conceptualization and Research Strategy for the Study of Ecological Aspects of the Quality of Life." *Social Indicators Research* 10.2 (February 1982): 133-52.

Millspaugh, Arthur C. "Bi-Partisanship and Vote Manipulation in Detroit." *National Municipal Review* 5 (October 1916): 620-26.

Niebuhr, R. "Ford's Five-Day Week Shrinks." *Christian Century* 9 June 1927: 713-14.

Nixon, J.W. "How Ford's Lowest-Paid Workers Live." *Social Service Review* 5 (March 1931): 37-46.

Pollard, Sidney. "Factory Discipline in the Industrial Revolution." *Economic History Review* 16 (December 1963): 254-71.

Porter, Harry Franklin. "Four Big Lessons from Ford's Factory." *System* 16 (June 1917): 639-46.

———. "Giving the Men a Share: What It's Doing for Ford." *System* 31 (March 1917): 262-70.

Reitell, Charles. "Machinery and Its Effects upon the Workers in the Automotive Industry." *The Annals* (November 1924): 37-43.

Scott, Emmet J. "Letters of Negro Migrants of 1916-1918." *The Journal of Negro History* 4 (1919): 291-340.

Shafer, J.F. "The Ford Stores, A New Departure in Retailing." *Harvard Business Review* April 1928.

Shelly, Cara L. "Second Baptist Church of Detroit, 1910-1946." *Michigan Historical Review* 17.1 (1991): 1-33.

Sly, David F,. and Peter S.K. Chi "Economic Development, Modernization, and Demographic Behavior." *The American Journal of Economics and Sociology* 31 (1972): 378-86.

Speek, Peter A. "The Psychology of Floating Workers." *AAAPSS* 69 (January 1917): 72-78.

"Standard of Living of Employees of Ford Motor Company in Detroit." *Monthly Labor Review* 30 (June 1930): 1204-52.

Thomas, Richard W. "The Detroit Urban League: 1916-1923." *Michigan History* 60 (Winter 1976): 315-38.

Vargas, Zaragosa. "Life and Community in the 'Wonderful City of the Magic Motor': Mexican Immigrants in 1920s Detroit." *Michigan Historical Review* 15.1 (1989): 47-68.

White, Walter F. "The Success of Negro Migration." *Crisis* 19 (January 1920): 112-15.

Dissertations, Theses, Typescripts

Bailer, Lloyd H. "Negro Labor in the Automobile Industry." Ph.D. dissertation, University of Michigan, 1943.

Carlson, Glen, E. "The Negro in the Industries of Detroit." Ph.D. dissertation, University of Michigan, 1929.

Chavis, John M.T. "James Couzens: Mayor of Detroit, 1919-1922." Ph.D. dissertation, Michigan State University, 1970.

Eckstein, Peter. "The Automobile in Michigan: A Case Study of Regional Development." Unpublished Manuscript, 1984.

Hathaway, Ellen C. "The Birth and Growth of Education in Highland Park." Master's Thesis, Wayne State University, 1949.

Lewis, David L. "History of Negro Employment in Detroit Area Automotive Plants of Ford Motor Company 1914-1941." A University of Michigan typescript essay, 1954.

Lowery, Joel John. "Labor Relations in the Automobile Industry During the Nineteen Twenties." Master's Thesis, Michigan State University, 1958.

Oestreicher, Richard F. "Solidarity and Fragmentation: Working People and Class Consciousness in Detroit, 1887-1895." Ph.D. dissertation, Michigan State University, 1979.

Peterson, Joyce Shaw. "A Social History of Automobile Workers Before Unionization, 1900-1933." Ph.D. dissertation, University of Wisconsin, 1976.

Thomas, Richard W. "From Peasant to Proletarian: The Formation and Organization of the Black Industrial Working Class, 1915-1945." Ph.D. dissertation, University of Michigan, 1976.

Ticknor, James. "Motor City: The Impact of the Automobile Industry upon Detroit, 1900-1975." Ph.D. dissertation, University of Michigan, 1978.

Government Documents

Americanization Committee of Detroit. *Articles of Association of the Americanization Committee of Detroit*, 1914.

Detroit Board of Commerce. *Information for Immigrants in Detroit, Michigan: Preparing to Be American Citizens*. Detroit, 1915.

Detroit Bureau of Governmental Research, Inc. *The Negro in Detroit*, 1926.

Detroit City Planning Commission. *Master Plan Reports: The People of Detroit*. Detroit, 1946.

Michigan Bureau of Labor Statistics. *Eighth Annual Report: A Canvas of Agricultural Implement and Iron Working Industries in Detroit*. Lansing, Mich., 1891.

Michigan Department of Labor. "Factory Inspection." *Thirty-seventh Annual Report*, Lansing, Mich., 1920.

Michigan Department of Labor. *Thirty-first Annual Report*. Lansing, Mich., 1914.

Michigan Department of Labor. *Thirty-second Annual Report*. Lansing, Mich., 1915.

U.S. Bureau of Education. *Proceedings: Americanization Conference*. Washington, D.C. 1919.

U.S. Bureau of Labor Statistics, Bulletin 438: *Wages and Hours of Labor in the Motor Vehicle Industry 1925*.

U.S. Congress. House of Representatives, Industrial Commission. *Report of the Industrial Commission on the Relations and Conditions of Capital and Labor Employed in Manufacturing and General Business*. House Document 183, 57th Congress, 1st session 1901.

U.S. Department of Commerce. Bureau of the Census. *Abstract of the Fifteenth Census of the United States: 1930.*

U.S. Department of Commerce. Bureau of the Census. *Abstract of the Fourteenth Census of the United States: 1920.*

U.S. Department of Commerce. Bureau of the Census. *Abstract of the Thirteenth Census of the United States: 1910.*

U.S. Department of Commerce. Bureau of the Census. *Fifteenth Census of the United States, 1930, Population, IV.*

U.S. Department of Commerce. Bureau of the Census. *Special Census of the Population of Highland Park, Michigan, November 15, 1915.*

U.S. Department of the Interior. Census Office. *Report on Vital and Social Statistics in the United States at the Eleventh Census: 1890.* 2 vols. Washington, D.C.: Government Printing Office, 1896.

U.S. Department of Labor. Bureau of Labor Statistics. *Wages and Hours of Labor in the Automobile Industry, 1922.* Bulletin No. 348, October 1923.

U.S. Department of Labor. Children's Bureau. *Minors in Automobile and Metal Manufacturing Industries in Michigan.* Bureau Publication No. 126, 1923.

Archives and Special Collections

Burton Historical Collection. Detroit Public Library: Detroit, Mich.

    Turner, Arthur, and Earl R. Moses. *Colored Detroit: A Brief History of Detroit's Colored Population and a Directory of Their Businesses, Organizations, Professions and Trades.* Detroit, 1924.

    Washington, Forrester B. *The Negro in Detroit: A Survey of the Conditions of a Negro Group in a Northern Industrial Center During the War Prosperity Period.* Detroit, 1920.

Ford Motor Company Archives. Dearborn, Mich.

Mayor's Papers. Detroit Public Library.

McGregor Library, Highland Park, Mich.

Michigan Historical Collection at Bentley Historical Library, Ann Arbor, Mich.

    Detroit Urban League Papers. Board of Directors Minutes and Papers 1916-50.

    Detroit Urban League Papers. Executive Secretary's General File from June 1916-June 1927.

    Papers of Arthur J. Tuttle. Americanization Committee of Detroit Papers 1914-31.

Newspapers

Detroit Evening News	1890–1930
Detroit Free Press	1890–1930
Detroit News	1890–1930
Detroit Saturday Night	1900–1910
Detroit Sunday News-Tribune	1890–1930
The Detroiter	1900–1920
Highland Park Times	1900–1917
Highland Parker	1917–1926
The New York Times	1890–1930

Index

CPSIA information can be obtained
at www.ICGtesting.com
Printed in the USA
FFOW03n1052040917
39503FF